The Life Within Her

D. DUQUETTE

To my childhood best friends. Near or far, our memories make life a little sweeter

CHAPTER ONE

We're five years into our marriage now. It's been nothing short of absolute bliss, but something has suddenly changed with Travis. He used to obsess over me, asking for sex almost every night. It's been a month since he's even touched me. I snuggle up to him and he rolls over yawning, signaling he's tired.

Is he having an affair? I'm twenty-three and I have a banging body. I've always been thin, with medium-sized perky breasts. I receive compliments all the time on how cute I dress or my rocking short haircut. When I was a little girl, I used to thank God for gracing me with a pretty face when I looked in the mirror. With my pin straight honey blonde hair and piercing green eyes, I knew a lot of females would kill for my all-natural beauty.

I started paying attention to Travis more than usual. I even grabbed his cellphone during one of his late-night trips to the bathroom, only to find he had a lock on it. After two failed attempts with what I thought his password might be, I quickly returned his phone to the nightstand in fear he'd catch me.

After a week of trying to uncover the details of a scandalous affair, I was convinced Travis was sick. His skin was flush and he itched a lot. Sometimes I would find him nodding off in exhaustion before noon and other times I would wake up listening to him vomit in our bathroom down the hall.

I tried to carry on as normal as possible and pretend like I didn't have a tornado of thoughts swirling around in my head. I went to work that day, rehearsing what I was going to say when I finally confronted Travis this evening. First, I would ask him if he was sick. If that got me nowhere, then I was going to accuse him of cheating on me.

When I arrived home, his truck was in the driveway. This was the norm ever since his landscape company stopped turning a profit over a year ago. I used to be the one who returned home early and had dinner waiting on the table when he walked through the door covered in dirt and smelling like fresh cut grass. Now I find him sitting on the couch watching television or playing video games. I'll admit it used to bother me because the trash would need emptying or dishes scrubbed, but now I have learned to shut my mouth. Through the years I've come to realize that Travis has a temper and some things just weren't worth fighting over.

I climbed the stone pavers to our house and opened the door. I called for Travis as I set my purse on the bench by the door, but he didn't respond. I wandered through the first floor, finding no sign of life. *God forbid he'd make dinner for once*. I climbed the stairs and called out his name again, but was met by silence. When I turned the corner into our bedroom, the door to our bathroom was open just far enough for me to see Travis' lifeless feet on the floor. I ran full speed, jumping through the crack in the door, careful not to step on him.

I screamed out in horror when I saw what laid before me. Travis was on his side, curled up with a needle hanging out of his arm. "Travis...Travis. Can you hear me?" He didn't seem to be breathing. I ran downstairs to retrieve my phone and dialed 9-1-1 right away. I sprinted back upstairs to Travis again.

"Shit," I mumbled to no one as I checked his pulse. I

couldn't feel anything on his wrist, so I moved to his neck. "No, no baby, please no." I heard commotion coming from downstairs and I bolted as fast as I could, almost crashing into one of the paramedics as I turned the corner at the bottom of the stairs.

"He's up here. Hurry, please!" I ran back up the stairs, sitting on our bed and pointing the paramedics towards the direction of our bathroom. I was out of breath now or maybe I was just hyperventilating. I turned my head away as they tried to resuscitate Travis...my whole world.

"Is this man your husband?" I heard a male voice ask. I lifted my head from my tear-soaked hands to see a police officer turning down the radio on his shoulder. He was handsome with chocolate brown hair and dark brown eyes. He looked to be about my age or maybe a few years older.

"Yes."

"Does he have a past history of drug abuse?"

"WHAT? No, never!"

"Well it appears your husband has overdosed."

"He doesn't do drugs!"

"Is he a diabetic?" he snickered. *Was he being sarcastic?* I studied his facial expression, which gave nothing away.

"No, although he's been acting sick lately."

"Okay. Can I have his full name and date of birth, please?" His entire demeanor lacked the empathy I so desperately needed right now, so I curled up into a ball on my bed as I listened to the paramedics in the bathroom.

"Ma'am? Ma'am," the officer continued, but I ignored him, not wanting to speak any further.

"You just sit tight, ma'am. Everything will be okay," he said after a minute.

A few moments passed when I heard Travis moaning in the bathroom and the first responders shuffling around. I sat up and saw Travis being put on the stretcher. As they strapped him down, he started swinging his hands which were now clenched into fists. He grabbed the EMT, holding him by his shirt. Travis yanked the man towards him. The EMT stumbled just before the police officer jumped in, pinning Travis' hands down. Travis began yelling and thrashing his head around. Spit was flying out of his mouth. I couldn't even make out the words he was shouting.

There were so many first responders around Travis now, I couldn't even see him. As they wheeled him by our bed I backed up until my back hit the wall. I was in complete shock. I had never seen this side of him. He was practically foaming at the mouth like a wild animal.

"Would you like to ride along in the ambulance?" the officer asked.

All I could do was shake my head in horror. I didn't want to be anywhere near that savage I called my husband.

I watched as the officer went to our bathroom. It was at that moment I realized I had my comforter drawn up to my chin, gripping the cotton until my knuckles were white. The officer returned with a plastic bag in his hand.

"W-what-what's that?" I asked, hearing myself stutter. My limbs were trembling.

"Drug paraphernalia. I'll take it with me."

I shook my head in denial. *This can't be real.*

"Ma'am."

"Stop calling me ma'am! What is in the bag?"

"I have a syringe, a baggy with white residue, a water bottle cap, cotton balls and a belt. What do you suppose all this is?" he asked impatiently. I wanted to smack him. I was just a low-class citizen to him, a druggie's wife.

"I don't know. I have no idea! We've been married for five years. He's my best friend and I know everything about him. Can you test that? You need to test it!"

"I don't need to. This is heroin. I see this stuff all the time," he said, shaking the bag in the air.

"Heroin?" I asked, my voice cracking.

"It's an opiate and it's highly addictive."

"What does it do?"

"Gets you high. He couldn't have hidden this from you. You had to have noticed changes."

"Yes, I told you...he seemed...sick. He slept a lot during the day and I heard him throw up once."

"Withdrawal symptoms."

"I've never even tried weed. Drugs make me feel dirty. Did you get it all?"

"I got it all."

"Can you search the rest of the house?" I pleaded.

"We don't do that," he answered, trying to stifle a grin.

"Can't you bring a dog in then or something?" I continued berating him with questions, even though he seemed to find humor in my lack of knowledge.

"No."

"Where are they taking my husband?"

"To the hospital until he is stable and then to jail."

"To jail? For what?"

"Possession of an illegal substance."

"So, I have to bail him out?"

"Well, you don't have to. Not if you don't want to."

"Then what happens?"

"If nobody bails him out, he will stay in jail until his court hearing."

I stood there with my arms crossed, shaking my head. I wanted to pull my hair out.

"Is that all?" the officer asked signaling his departure.

"That's all," I replied, quietly. When he turned to walk away, I got off the bed to follow him down the stairs. He turned to me before walking through the front door.

"Are you going to be okay?" he asked, sounding genuine.

I hesitated, but gave him the answer I knew he wanted to hear.

"I'll be fine, thank you."

"Have a good night," he said and with that he was gone.

I slid down the door and did what anybody would do when they found out they were married to a completely different person than what they had ever imagined. I cried.

I was mad as hell. I felt betrayed. My manicured life as I knew it was tainted. If you had asked me yesterday how my life was, I would have told you perfect. I have a dream job as the head of the accounting department for our local university where I'm pulling in a six-figure annual income. I had worked there all throughout college, so when I graduated and they asked me to come aboard, it was a no-brainer. We were understaffed as it was and then my favorite co-worker went out on maternity leave. While she was home changing diapers and wiping drool, the manager was diagnosed with some rare form of cancer. She up and left us that same day. Some people's misfortunes are other's fortunes and that was the story for me. I fell right into the manager's position and thrived at it. I had a cute house. It was nothing spectacular, but I was proud of it. I drove a sleek new Toyota Avalon and I was content. I even thought I had a great husband.

Life had always come easy to me. When I wanted something, I went for it and I usually got it. Tonight was the first time I felt like I wanted a new life away from Travis. I decided I wasn't going to post his bail. He was going to sit in jail where he couldn't do drugs and wait until his court hearing.

****

The next day I marched into the Human Resources office with a pep in my step. I needed to fill out paperwork to have ten percent of my paycheck go into another account, one Travis never knew about. It was the one my parents had set up for me when I was just a baby.

My mother faithfully saved every penny I had ever received since I was born. Birthday money, Easter and Christmas. She presented it to me when I graduated from high school. There was just over ten thousand dollars in the account then. I remember thinking I was rich and vowing never to touch it unless there was a serious emergency. There was no emergency, yet anyway, but I had to prepare myself for one.

When I arrived home, there was a message for me on our answering machine. It was Travis. I laughed to myself, knowing full well he could've called my cellphone. Instead he called our home phone knowing I would be at work. *What a coward.*

"Hey. Fitzy bailed me out. You can't begin to know how sorry I am. I'll explain everything when I get home. I'm going to a detox center for seven days. I promise you, I'm done. This will never happen again. Please forgive me! You're the greatest part of my life and I hope you always know that."

What was there to explain?

I played the message again as I sat at my dining room table. With my forehead pressed against the coolness of the glass, I wept. *I cannot believe this is happening. Travis is in a detox center?* I was ready to start the next chapter of my life, like having children, for starters. I could never bring a child into this world with a drug addicted father. I felt like the rug was swept out from underneath my feet.

I wasn't going forward in life, I was going backwards. I snapped. I grabbed the vase of flowers on the table and threw them against the floor. I whipped our wedding pictures off the walls one by one and hurled them across the room. I didn't stop there. I went to every room in the house, destroying every sentimental piece that represented our life together. Our life was broken. I was completely deceived. When I was done, I reached for the blanket in front of me, curled up on the floor in a fetal position and cried myself to sleep.

When I awoke the next morning and started to get ready for work, I tried desperately to ignore the mess I had made and carried on like there wasn't a mountain of pain sitting heavily on my heart. I put on that smile that everyone wanted to see and went about my day.

I could hardly concentrate at work. I declined my co-worker's offer to take a walk around campus during our lunch break. *Ugh, perhaps some fresh air would do me some good.* Maybe I could lean on her shoulder as we walked and tell her everything. But I was in no shape to walk. I hadn't eaten a single thing today.

On my ride home, I chastised myself for not being a productive employee today. I was so distracted I would have to work extra hard tomorrow if I didn't want anyone to notice I was falling behind.

I didn't feel like doing anything right now except lay in bed, but all I could think about as I stood outside my front door was the giant mess behind it. I turned the key and opened the door, feeling ashamed of my behavior the night before. *This wasn't me. I don't destroy things.*

I went to our cleaning closet, retrieving the broom and dustpan along with our vacuum and started tidying up my mess. I decided to go through every drawer, cabinet and nook and cranny in my house in search of more drugs. This is all I did during that week without Travis, wondering in the back of my mind what was going to happen to our marriage. Travis made it clear he still wanted to be with me, *but did I want to be with him?*

CHAPTER TWO

Seven days came and went from the time Travis had left the message on our machine. I was anxious at work all day. When I arrived home, there was still no sign of Travis. I had bought groceries to make a nice dinner, bought fresh flowers and told myself I couldn't just give up. I gave Travis my word five years ago on that altar, through the good times and the bad. This was just a bad time in our lives, but things were going to get better.

I heard the door click open and I practically jumped out of my heels. Turning, I saw Travis coming towards the kitchen through our side door.

"Hey," I said, quietly. He looked exhausted. I hated to see him this way. I did love him, I guess I never stopped. I was just upset.

"Hey. I guess this means you're talking to me?"

"Of course I'm going to talk to you, Travis."

"You didn't come to the hospital. You never came to the police station. You could've called the detox center all week..."

"I just needed time. You have no idea how betrayed I feel."

"I can imagine," he said, walking over to me and wrapping me in his embrace. "I'm so sorry." His voice was shaky and he began to cry.

"How long?" I asked, trying my best to hold back my own tears. I had never seen Travis this broken before. I had never even seen him cry.

"Heroin?"

"Are there other drugs?"

"No."

"Well how long have you been doing heroin then?"

"This time around or when did I first start?"

"I didn't realize there was a difference. So, this wasn't your first time?"

"No. I've been using on and off since I was sixteen."

I was speechless. *Sixteen*? I felt the blade of deception deepen. I pushed away from him.

"How could you go all this time and never tell me?"

"Cora," he said, running his hands through his hair in frustration. "You're sheltered. You never so much as tried marijuana. You never would've married me if you knew I was a recovering heroin addict. You would have never taken me home to your do-good mom and your father, a pastor. We would've ended the day I told you. I selfishly had to have you because you kept me from relapsing."

"Relapsing?"

"I never wanted anything more than heroin...until the day I met you. You showed me that staying clean far outweighed the life I was used to living."

"And now? Why now?"

"Business has slowed and I'm going to have to claim a loss this year, while you're pulling in six figures. Do you know how incompetent that makes me feel?"

"I'm the reason you relapsed, because I work hard providing for us? Do you hear yourself? It's just a cop out, using me as your scapegoat. You know what's actually worse than your empty excuse? The fact that you use that money that makes you feel less of a man to feed your addiction," I seethed, laughing sarcastically. I started to walk away. I couldn't stand to look at this frail man I thought was so strong.

"Wait Cora! What about us?"

"I feel like I don't even know you! What do you expect me to say?"

"That you won't give up on me."

"I just need some time to wrap my head around all of this."

I grabbed my keys and got into Travis' pick-up truck. I loved his truck. I was higher off the ground compared to my Avalon, which made me feel safe. I needed that right now.

I drove to one of my favorite roads in Massachusetts. It was a single lane dirt road that wasn't maintained by the town, so at the beginning was a sign warning you to drive at your own risk. It was a winding road that followed the outskirts of our local pond. The sand had eroded in some parts where my tires touched the water. When I came to a spot where I could pull off, I parked the truck and sat there thinking.

When I realized I had never checked Travis' truck for drugs, I started opening compartments and using the flashlight on my phone to check underneath the seats. I was making myself crazy. I didn't want to live this kind of life. I just wanted to go back to the way I thought things were.

After I drove down just about every road in our town, I returned home. When I walked through the door, Travis was out cold in our living room recliner. I checked his arm for a needle and fell to my knees crying.

"Cora, what's wrong?"

"I'm standing here not knowing if you're sleeping or dead.

I hate this! I don't trust you anymore! How can I not trust the one person I have bared my soul to?"

Travis pulled me onto his lap and held me. Sobs wracked my entire body. My heart was broken.

"I promise that's the last time."

"When I found you in our bathroom, I thought you were dead. Do you know how scared I was?"

"I'll do whatever it takes. Please don't give up on me."

I think I cried every possible tear my eye ducts held. After what seemed like forever, my head hurt and my face stung. I was exhausted. Travis carried me up the stairs to our bed.

"Let's make a baby," he whispered in my ear.

"I thought you weren't ready yet," I said, completely shocked by his words.

"That was when we met. I want one now...so badly. I think being a dad will keep me sober."

I had always dreamt of having children. Travis was the only reason I wasn't a mom. *What if he was right? What if having a baby would make him want more out of life than turning to drugs? Maybe this was our answer, a way of fixing things. A baby could give both our lives a new meaning. Perhaps I was being credulous or just plain stupid and should think this through more.* His eyes were pleading for an answer and crazy or not, I poured all my faith in him into my response.

"Yes," I breathed. I so desperately wanted Travis to stay sober and wanted a baby more than anything. Boy or girl, it didn't matter. From that night on we started trying to conceive. After three months, our dreams came true. We were both overjoyed.

It wasn't long after that I started feeling nauseous every day. I would wake up feeling fine, but as soon as I drank my coffee or ate anything, I felt that ball in the pit of my stomach. I never actually threw up, I'd just feel sick all day. I thought of all the women that had eight or twelve children. *How did they do it?*

I was just coming out of my nauseous phase when I returned home from work to find Travis in his truck, slumped over his steering wheel. I frantically grabbed for the handle and jiggled it in my hand, but his truck was locked. I fumbled for my phone in my purse, dialing 9-1-1 right away. I put my face up to the glass and banged my fists on his window as hard as I could. His body remained lifeless. I started screaming, desperately begging for help to arrive. I saw a yellowish black goo oozing out of Travis' mouth.

*No…please no…*was the mantra I played in my head until the paramedics arrived. I stood there in horror as if someone hit the replay button. The police officers smashed Travis' window, gaining access to the truck and stabilized his hand as they inserted something into his nose, which turned out to be nasal spray. And then again. After a moment Travis reared his head back and the unleashed beast made an appearance. I held my hands up over my eyes. I couldn't watch anymore. It was all so incredibly disturbing.

"Ma'am, your husband will be okay." I felt arms around me. "Let's go have a seat on your steps over here."

"Why can't he stop? Why is he doing this to us?"

"I'm so sorry, ma'am."

"I'm pregnant with his baby. How the hell is he supposed to be a father?"

"It'll be okay."

It wasn't going to be okay! It was like I was hitting a rewind button. I denied a ride along with Travis to the hospital. *Repeat again.* I begged the officers to turn my house upside down looking for more drugs. *Repeat. Repeat. REPEAT!* I went to work the next day and upped my contribution to my secret savings account. Then I returned to my desk and cried.

I didn't understand after all these years, how Travis could just throw our relationship away for some drugs. *Was I blind? What pain was he trying to numb?* I never should've run away with him. I never should've gotten married after knowing him for three months. *What was I thinking?* I was only eighteen, dumb and in love.

I rubbed my stomach and whispered to chicklet. "Chicklet, I love you. I loved you the moment I saw those two lines on the pregnancy test. I've never experienced a feeling quite like it before. That's why this is going to be the hardest thing I have ever had to do. I cannot bring you into a broken marriage where your father puts heroin before you...before us. He will ruin you the way he has ruined me. I'm doing this for both of us."

And so I carried out with the most heinous thing I have ever had to do. I called an abortion clinic over a hundred miles away and made the next day appointment to murder my own flesh and blood. I had to do it before I gave it another thought. I knew what I was doing was wrong. After all, there was adoption, but I couldn't risk Travis finding out and trying to gain custody of this innocence we created. I sobbed the entire ride there and was hardly able to see the road in front of me.

I walked through those doors with my womb full, full of love for this tiny creature I had never met and when I left, I was empty both inside my uterus and my heart. It was all too easy to make such a terrible life altering decision. I was pro-life, never pro-choice. *Who was I?* I was a murderer. I stopped that heartbeat. I exited through the front doors and threw up in the parking lot. I climbed into my car, pulling down the visor mirror to check my mouth for leftover vomit. I couldn't stand to look at the person staring back at me.

Where would I go from here? How could I carry on? I wanted desperately to run away, but I drove back to the only place I could call home. My life was falling apart and I didn't know whether this was rock bottom or if there was more falling.

I went to work the next day and carried on like I had to. I went into the Human Resources office again.

"Hi Cora. What can I help you with today?"

"I'd like to change the percentage I debit into my direct deposit savings account."

"Again?"

"Yes."

"Friend to friend speaking, is there something going on that I should know about?"

"Yes and no, but more no than yes. If my husband calls, please tell him I took a demotion." I watched her eye me suspiciously, confusion clearly sprawled across her face as she grabbed the paperwork for me to fill out...again.

Last night I had thoughtfully calculated our monthly bills in order to afford to keep our lifestyle, along with storing any extra money for me, not for Travis to spend on drugs. This ought to really throw a curveball at his appetite for heroin.

I devised this plan. I wanted out, but I would hold onto my job and my marriage until I couldn't take it anymore...until my skin was crawling and I was ready to pull my own hair out. I was mentally capable of handling a great deal, which would help bide my time until I had enough money to leave.

See, I would deposit fifty percent of my weekly earnings into my secret account. I knew Travis would catch on the first week this change in my income disbursement went through. I was terrible at lying, so while Travis was in detox again, I was going to think up some good lies.

CHAPTER THREE

Travis was bailed out again. I haven't a clue who bailed him out this time. *Was it Fitzy again? No, unless he's an idiot...which he is. Maybe Fitzy did heroin also. Maybe he was Travis' dealer.* My thoughts continued to run away from me.

Like clockwork, seven days after Travis was in detox, he walked through our side door looking unkempt. I was embarrassed to call myself his wife.

"Hi," I said, not even wanting to deal with him. I cut right to the chase. "Seven days in detox didn't work last time. How do you expect it to work this time?"

"That's all they'll give me."

"Well who the hell decides that after seven days, you're ready to leave?"

"I don't know."

"Well I'm going to find out!" I declared, pushing my chair back and standing up. "Look at you, you're a mess! You need help. Seven days is bullshit! Tell me, were you ready to leave?"

"I don't know, Cora," he answered, breaking our eye contact and looking at the floor.

"I don't know means no. What's the name of this detox

center?"

"In the Midst. What, are you going to call them or something?" he scoffed.

"No. I'm driving down there and I'm going to find out why you aren't getting more help!"

"I'm going to shower," he mumbled, walking past me like a zombie. He wasn't my Travis anymore. My lungs were begging for air. I jumped into my car and punched the name of the detox center into my phone. I knew exactly where it was since I drove by it every time I headed out of town.

I expected it to be run down and dirty, but to my surprise it was really nice. When I reached the double doors, they were locked. *What kind of detox center was closed during the day?* I searched around, finding a button next to the door labeled **CALL**. I pressed on it.

"Hello. How may I help you?" A young female's voice came over the speaker.

"Are you open?"

"Of course. We never close, miss. Is there something I can help you with?"

"I need to talk to someone about my husband."

"Is he a patient here?"

"He was. He was just discharged from here. Travis Cavanaugh. He's not ready to be home yet, though. He's recovering from heroin."

"What do you mean he's not ready?"

"He was only here seven days. That's not enough!"

Ugh, what was it going to take to speak with someone face to face instead of talking to a wall on the side of a building? What the hell was this place?

"That's probably all your insurance company would pay for. If you fight it, most of them will give you two additional days."

"What? How are you supposed to put a one size fits all on something like drug addiction? That's ludicrous!"

"I completely agree. A lot of times they're not ready to leave, but we have to kick them out. They relapse and come back to us again. That's health insurance for you."

"What's the point of giving addicts any hope at all if you just pull the plug and push them out after seven or nine days?"

"I don't make the rules, I just do what is asked of me. Your husband is lucky they had a spot for him here. Most times we have to deny people because there are no beds available. I'm a nurse, so I naturally want to help people. The hardest thing I have to do is have someone before me asking for help to get clean and I have to tell them no. My heart breaks every day for these people."

"I don't get it. Why?"

"We're in the midst of a major drug epidemic. There's not enough detox centers."

In the Midst.

"Well there's no point in opening more facilities around here when these people only get seven days to completely change their lives around. Ridiculous! Thanks for your help."

"No problem and stay positive. What your husband needs right now is a good support system."

"Thanks," I muttered as I turned to leave. *Poor Travis, having to leave even if he wanted to stay.* I drove back home with a heavy heart, begging my own self for forgiveness. I found Travis laying on the couch staring up at the ceiling. He sat up when I entered the room.

"Where'd you go? I came back downstairs and you were gone."

"I told you, the detox facility. I wasn't joking. I went for a drive after to clear my head. I want you to get better, Travis. I'll do whatever it takes. I hate seeing you like this!"

"I'm trying."

"Are you thinking about heroin right now?" I asked, not sure I wanted to know the answer.

"Every day. I don't want to be like this. It has a hold over me. I promise when our baby comes, everything will be better."

I put my head down. I couldn't even look him in the eyes when I lied.

"I lost the baby Travis. I had a miscarriage."

"WHAT? WHEN? Why didn't you tell me?"

"I was so afraid that if I told you the moment you walked through that door, you would turn to heroin again. I'm traumatized! I can't do this anymore!"

"Did you miscarry because of me?"

"I don't know, maybe. I wasn't eating. I was so stressed out. It obviously wasn't meant to be. Everything happens for a reason, right?"

His bottom lip was trembling and it looked like he was on the verge of tears.

"Since we're being so honest, I decided I can't run the accounting department right now. I told them I have way too much going on in my home life. I can't even concentrate. I'm a mess right now. I have my job back when I want it. I just need to get a mental check. Okay?" I fibbed.

"Did you take a pay cut?"

"Of course I did, Travis. I purposely demoted myself. I had to! Are you even listening to me?"

"It's not enough money, Cora. You have to take your job back as head. We can't afford this house, your car, my truck."

Clearly Travis wasn't listening to me.

"I make more than enough! I already did out the calculations. Maybe we have to watch every penny for a little while, but we'll make it through."

I was secretly smiling on the inside. I wasn't stupid. Our new budget just wasn't enough to keep up with Travis' dirty habit.

"It's not enough," he repeated.

"What about you, Travis? If your landscaping business isn't helping us, then maybe it's time to close those doors and find something new."

"I'm not in the right state of mind to work right now. I need to do me for a little while."

Oh yeah? Me too.

CHAPTER FOUR

Flash forward six years now and Travis is still working on himself while I sit back and pray this longest stretch of the past nine months is a sign of full recovery. It's not like I've even asked him if he's staying sober because I wouldn't believe him anyway. He lost my trust that first night in our bathroom all those years ago and I've never been able to get it back. He fooled me once, shame on him and again when I got pregnant. Well that was shame on me. Now...now maybe I'm staying just to avoid adding divorce to my list of offenses.

I've tried desperately to fall in love with Travis again. I even googled ideas on how to fall back in love. I'm pathetic. I forced myself to hug and kiss him. We've even made love, but it just wasn't the same anymore.

Six...whole...years feeling like this. I'm almost thirty years old now and Travis is still "working on himself". Nothing has changed except he's built a nasty reputation for himself. He hasn't had a job and no aspiration to find one. He doesn't help at home and he doesn't love me anymore. At least, I don't think he does. He has consistently made it a point to tell me it's time for me to take my job back as head of my department. Little does he know I have sat back and watched my savings account grow. If he ever found out I lied about my demotion, he'd be furious. He looks at me and all he sees is dollar signs.

I look around our house now and it's practically empty. Travis has sold everything from our DVD collection to our DVD player. My beloved coin collection went missing and my jewelry box, well let's just say it doesn't hold a single piece of my jewelry anymore. I thank God every day I was smart enough to hide the ruby ring my grandfather had given me for my sixteenth birthday. And Travis' motorcycle, I swear he dumped it on purpose so he could get the insurance money. He seemed all too happy when that check came in the mail.

I'm not stupid. I just choose to keep my mouth shut. My plan I devised all those years ago is the only thing that keeps me going. It was my fault Travis pawned my possessions anyway. I was the one who deposited just enough money into our account to pay our bills. I didn't want to keep playing this game, it didn't make me feel good about myself. I was raised to tell the truth, not to be a sneaky and underhanded.

Today was my thirtieth birthday, as well as the day before Easter. It was clear Travis had forgotten my special day, but it wasn't the first time. I decided I was going to put my entire heart into making it a wonderful Easter day. I came home from work, cooked dinner for me and Travis, then ventured back out to buy Travis a few gifts for his Easter basket. When I returned home, I could see him through the window sitting on our couch with a tourniquet wrapped tightly around his arm. I watched the entire time. I wanted to see for myself, through my very own eyes, that all these months of sobriety meant nothing to him. I wasn't angry anymore and I wasn't sad either, I was just...done. It's been too long that I've felt empty inside. I have no love for myself and I certainly have no love for my husband.

His eyes rolled back, his head resting on the back of the couch and that was my cue to go. I snuck inside, careful not to make any noise. Although I'm not sure there was much Travis could do to stop me if he found me packing. I grabbed my empty jewelry box and ran my fingers over my grandmother's name engraved on the back. *Someday I will fill this with the most beautiful jewelry.*

I moved to my dresser, unzipping the biggest duffle bag I owned and shoved as many everyday clothes as I could possibly fit, along with a few pairs of shoes. I crept towards the side door. I took one last look at Travis still passed out on the couch and said a tiny little prayer in my head. *May someday you get better. May someday you find a beautiful woman you love more than heroin. May you forgive me for leaving you and may you never ever come looking for me. Amen.*

I threw everything in the bed of Travis' truck. His truck was in my name and didn't have any payments left on the loan. Everything was in my name, one of Travis' ideas he thought of when he read about one lawsuit ruining a small business owner for life. I thought it was ridiculous at the time, all the paperwork I had to fill out transferring ownership, but now I think it was brilliant.

I used the backup camera in the truck to guide my way back to our six-person tow behind camper. I had never actually done this by myself, but I helped on numerous occasions and felt confident enough in hitching our camper up to his truck. My thoughts were that if I took our camper too, I could stay in the Walmart parking lot while I drove across the country, figuring out where the hell I could start a new life. *Safety latch down, plug camper lights into the back of the truck, hook up the chains and make sure nothing is dangling too low to the ground. Check, check and check!*

I dialed 9-1-1 as I pulled out of the driveway, giving the dispatcher my address and telling him about a possible overdose. I passed the police cruisers right before I reached the main road. I had to call. If I left right now and found out later that Travis had died, I'd never be able to forgive myself.

My chest hurt as I reached the highway. It was then I realized I had been holding my breath. I felt lightheaded. Maybe I should pull over. *No, no time to waste...I need to get away.* I was never going to let him hurt me ever again. I was such a fool. My parents would be ashamed of me. I let him strip me of my pride, my confidence and every moral I had ever known. I don't even know who I am anymore. Just a wife who gave twelve years to her heroin addicted husband.

I don't love him anymore. I haven't loved him for some time, but I don't believe in divorce. Through thick and thin. I gave him my word! I stood up on that altar in front of my closest friends and family and told him I would always be there. I'm a liar, I'm a fake and a phony. What I believe in is happiness. It's no longer a term I know. I have spent so many years not believing in divorce that I completely forgot what it was like to be happy.

I ache to smile. It wasn't always this way. As I drove, checking in my review mirror from time to time, I thought back to the days we were happy. Travis would bring me coffee at work or surprise me with flowers on the table when I returned home. Sometimes he would even plan out an entire romantic weekend away. I used to think I was the luckiest girl in the world.

I checked my watch. I had been driving for three hours. Surely now I could take a quick nap and be on my way. I pulled off into a rest area and parked the truck. I was amongst a row of sleeping truck drivers in their big rigs. I laid down on the bench seat, using my purse as a pillow. I softly sang happy birthday to myself as I wept in self-pity. I closed my eyes and pictured a cake with a single candle I was to blow out using one wish. My wish was simple. I dreamt for new beginnings.

****

I instantly jumped up. It was light out. I looked at my phone and realized I had slept four hours. I had to get out of here and fast. It was raining now. *Oh no, my belongings are in the bed of the truck.* It crossed my mind for an instant that all my possessions had been stolen, but there everything was, jewelry box and all, in broad daylight. I grabbed everything, squeezing out what water I could before placing everything on the floor in the front passenger side. *I guess I don't have a change of clothes for today.*

I ran into the rest stop, using the restroom before placing an order for a hot coffee and a bagel with vegetable cream cheese. I foolishly grabbed for my debit card out of habit and then apologized to the cashier, grabbing it back out of her hand before she swiped it and gave Travis a clue into my whereabouts.

"Forgot I had cash," I explained, trying to justify my odd behavior. "Keep the change."

"Happy Easter!" she smiled.

Easter? Oh, right...Easter.

I decided I would go see my parents first. I hadn't seen them in three years, which filled my heart with so much guilt. Travis' addiction had taken its toll on my appearance and I knew it. I had lost quite a bit of weight or so my doctor said. When I looked in the mirror, my eyes were sunken in with dark bags under them. I looked like a druggie myself. I had stayed away from my parents because they'd ask questions and I knew they didn't deserve to be lied to. Just my voice during our phone calls over the years would trigger a string of questions about my happiness. They knew me better than anyone.

That's why I will go to them, spill my guts out and pray they have an answer for me. I punched their address into my GPS. Fifteen hours to go. I drove all day and by night fall I could feel my eyes drooping. I was in Illinois, the last state to go through until I was back into the familiar territory of Iowa. I pulled off into a rest stop like I had the night before, only this time I locked up the truck, headed to the camper and used the light on my cellphone to make the dinette table into a bed. I fished around for the sheets and comforter. I wanted to feel some sort of normalcy. I fell asleep dreaming of being in my parents' arms again.

When I woke the next morning, I knew I only had three hours to go. This ride would be a breeze. When I passed the border to Iowa, I read the sign, Field of Opportunities. *God, I pray that's true*! My heart began to beat faster as I turned onto my parent's street. I slowed as I neared their house, seeing both their vehicles home. I drove past. I thought I could do this, but talking about abortion with a pastor...my dad would never forgive me. Maybe he would forgive me, but he most certainly would never look at me the same again.

I was nearing my best friend's house from childhood. There was a For Sale sign out front with a truck in the driveway. I wondered if her mom, Sherri, still lived there. I pulled in the driveway. If I knocked on the door and Sherri no longer lived there, then at least I could use the driveway to turn around. The roads were narrow in this neck of the woods and I wasn't good at maneuvering the truck with the camper attached. I parked, got out and headed towards the side door. I knocked a couple times and then rang the doorbell for good measure. After a minute, a man with a little girl wrapped around his leg opened the door.

"Hi, does Sherri still live here?"

"No, I'm afraid not. She's been moved to a nursing

home...early Alzheimer's."

"Oh my! I'm so sorry, I had no idea. How is her daughter Maura?"

"She moved to California...married now and in the fashion industry."

"Oh wow!"

"I'm sorry, how do you know Sherri and Maura?"

"I was Maura's best friend growing up. Sherri was like my second mom. We lost touch a long time ago."

The man gazed at me with a confused look. I wondered what in the world he was thinking.

"Cora?"

My heart beat faster upon hearing my name. I studied his face; I'd recognize that smile anywhere.

"Weston? Oh my gosh, I can't believe I didn't recognize you!"

Maura's stepbrother.

Maura's dreamy stepbrother, whom I spent half my childhood following around like a lost puppy. Weston was mischievous, but sweet...comical, but thoughtful. He was the first one to run and get me a Band-Aid when I fell rollerblading and scraped my knee in this very driveway. The only one who I saw shake his head right before I was about to jump out of the bale door in the horse barn when my brother and his friends egged me on. Weston's silent plea not to jump was the only thing that stopped me. The same Weston who had every girl in our neighborhood wanting a slice of his attention.

"I definitely didn't recognize you...you've grown up!" he smiled, snapping me out of my thoughts.

"Officially thirty. An old woman now."

"Ouch, easy on the old. I'm soon to be thirty-four."

"And who is this?" I asked, looking at the sweet little girl staring up at me. She was beautiful, with caramel brown curly hair, light brown eyes and tan skin.

"This is my daughter Olivia."

"Hi Olivia!" I said, watching her smile and shy away behind Weston's leg.

"So what brings you back? Are you visiting your parents for Easter? I haven't talked to them in quite some time, although I see them out doing yard work together."

"Yeah, they're still madly in love. They've been married over forty years now."

I let the silence grow between us before realizing Weston had asked why I was home. *Should I tell him I am visiting for Easter or should I just be honest?* I wanted a fresh start. I didn't want to lie anymore.

"I'm not home for Easter. I'm actually here because I ran into some trouble a long time ago and I tried to stay and make it right, but I don't think I can. I guess I'm running away from it." I looked out at the driveway, too nervous to look Weston in the eye. "I thought I could tell my parents everything and maybe they could offer some kind of advice for me, but when I reached their driveway, I just couldn't pull in. I chickened out, so here I am. I mean, I saw the For Sale sign in the front yard and thought maybe I could catch up with Sherri again, but apparently you live here now."

"No, no. I'm just helping Sherri out. I put that sign out today. Sherri's money ran out and now the nursing home has to liquidate all her assets. I have thought about buying this place. I have so many great childhood memories here and Olivia practically lives here. Sherri would take her on the weekends. It's just, I'd have to start over with new clients and all."

"I hear you. How much are you selling it for anyway?"

"Why, are you interested?"

"I don't know. Maybe? I do need somewhere to put my camper. I'm kind of homeless. I own a home, but I have no intentions of ever going back there."

"Where is 'there'?"

I looked at Weston, eyeing him suspiciously. *Could telling him do any harm?*

"Massachusetts," I blurted out before I could give it a second thought.

"I heard there's a drug epidemic going on there right now."

Ding. Ding. Ding.

I just nodded my head. It was a shame a beautiful state was getting such a bad reputation.

"So, you mean to tell me you just drove all the way from Massachusetts by yourself with that RV and your truck?" he asked. He cocked his head sideways as if he found this information most peculiar.

I shrugged my shoulders, trying my best to smile.

"Olivia, can you go play downstairs please. Daddy is going to talk to Cora here for a few minutes, okay?"

"Okay, Daddy," she replied, hopping through the kitchen. I watched her until she turned the corner and I could no longer see her. *Ah, to be young again.*

"Come on in. I'm sure you'd like to take a stroll down memory lane."

"Sure, I'd love that!"

"Can I get you some water?"

"No thank you, I'm fine. I looked around as I walked through the entryway into the kitchen which led to the living room. The house was gorgeous. Sherri loved decorating with a rustic country theme. The salt box style home had vaulted ceilings with a giant fireplace in the middle.

"What do you think? Just as you remember it?"

"Yes, it's beautiful...still takes my breath away."

We headed upstairs to the balcony that overlooked the living room.

"So, what are you running away from?"

I winced and closed my eyes. I didn't think Weston would ask me such a personal question. I started sweating.

"My husband," I whispered, afraid my voice might fail me.

I walked on, stopping by the bathroom and looking in. The green and blue rug had been replaced with tan colored tile.

"Did he hurt you?"

I paused, turning back around to face him.

"Yes, but not physically." *Deep breath.* "He's addicted to heroin, Weston."

"It's none of my business, but I mean...it's through thick and thin. He obviously has a problem and isn't leaving him going to make it worse?"

"Ask me how long."

"How long what?" Weston asked, placing his hands on his hips.

"Ask me how long I have been supportive through his fight with his addiction."

"How long?"

"Seven years. Now ask me how many times I have found him nearly dead and had to call 9-1-1."

"How many times?"

"Thirty-four times," I said, shuddering. "Do you want to do the math with me? Thirty-four times over seven years..."

He crossed his arms, shaking his head no. I would spare Weston the details like those days I called more than once. Every cop in my town was familiar with my face. They knew my name and they knew my address.

"I'm done. I'm not just a little done, I'm one hundred percent without a doubt DONE!" I rambled on, knowing if I shot Weston's until death do us part bullshit down right now, he wouldn't speak another word on it. "Truthfully, I don't believe in divorce, but I've battled the thick and thin thing, trust me. I don't even know what happiness is anymore. I feel like I'm under this dark cloud." Tears managed to sit on my eyelids as I tried desperately to swallow them away. "My life has been raining for so long and leaving that house and him, it's the first time I felt like maybe I could feel again. I am numb. I just...I don't know," I said, snaking my arms around my waist and glancing out the window that overlooked the backyard.

After a long pause, Weston let out a sigh.

"Sorry to put all this out there on you. It's just, I don't want to be judged and I'm so tired of lying to everybody. I would wear this fake empty smile to work, grocery shopping and even at home with my husband. I want to know what it's like to tell the truth again. I know you're still judging me anyway and that's okay..."

"I am not."

"Of course you are."

"Did you know he did drugs when you married him?"

"No!"

"Then it's not your fault."

"I married him so young and too fast. I didn't give myself enough time to get to know him. If I could go back..." I said, with tears springing to my eyes again. I wiped them away before they could fall.

"You would do things differently," Weston said, finishing my sentence.

"Yes."

I was the definition of pathetic. Here I was, pouring my

heart out to Weston, whom I hardly knew now. I was so engrossed in Travis and work that I never made an outlet of friends. It was now more than ever I wish I had a ride or die. I walked back down the stairs. Olivia emerged from the basement asking Weston for food.

"Well it was nice seeing you again..."

"Where are you going to go?" he asked, concerned.

"Oh, I don't know. Walmart lets you sleep in their parking lot for free. I was thinking about hopping around until I can figure out where I am going to settle down, you know?"

"Not really. It still gets pretty cold here at night. Living in your camper wouldn't be ideal until at least another month."

I just looked at him not knowing what to say.

"I need to get some food for Olivia. Would you like to come along? I mean...it is Easter after all and nobody should be alone on Easter."

It took all of ten seconds to think about my answer. I was starving and lunch seemed innocent enough.

"Sure, lunch sounds great! Can I park my truck and camper behind the house?" I dug into my pocket and retrieved my keys.

"You think he'll come looking for you?"

"I don't know. He's either in jail or detox right now. It's probably overkill, but I just don't want to draw any extra attention from anyone."

"Okay."

"Just don't watch me. I'm pretty terrible at backing up the camper."

Weston let out a chuckle. "You put Olivia in her car seat," he said, handing me his keys and taking mine, "and I'll go park your truck and camper. Okay?"

Phew.

"Okay."

"Go with Cora now, Olivia. Daddy will be right with you."

I held out my hand to Olivia and she cautiously took it. Her whole hand wrapped around one of my fingers. The contact brought instant warmth to my heart. It was a feeling I hadn't felt in quite some time. I picked Olivia up, buckling her in.

"What's your favorite movie?" I asked her.

"Trolls," she replied. I had never even heard of it. I typed Trolls soundtrack into my phone and YouTube was the first link to pop up. I clicked on it and watched Olivia's face light up with the first song that came on. I watched Olivia smile. She was a beautiful little girl. By the time Weston climbed into his truck, Olivia and I were dancing to the second song.

"What's going on here?"

"Trolls," I replied, shrugging my shoulders.

"I see you already found the way to my daughter's heart. This movie is her favorite. She watches it almost every night. Oh...by the way, I should warn you Olivia has lice. That's why she's with me this week. She usually goes next door to my neighbor's house, but all the kids she watches have lice, so she refused to watch any of our children until they are bug free. I took her to Urgent Care this morning and they gave me the name of a shampoo I could buy and told me to cut her hair real short. I've been contemplating all day on what I want to do. I called the other mother who drops her two kids there every day, but they're both boys so a short haircut isn't an issue. Olivia has those beautiful brown curls and they remind me of her mother. I'd just hate to cut them off."

I opened my mouth to speak, then paused a moment to think. *These curls remind Weston of Olivia's mother? Well, who IS her mother and where is she?* I chickened out on asking him and instead turned around to look at Olivia again. It *would* be a shame to cut those curls off.

"I know they'll grow back. I'm just...I don't know. It feels wrong," Weston said.

"You don't have to cut her hair. I mean, it will be much easier if you do. It'll take more time if you don't, but no way! I used to be a nanny and the little girl, she was five, had beautiful long blonde hair. Her mother had never given her a haircut and it was well past her butt. Anyway, she refused to give her daughter a short haircut like the school had suggested when they found out she had lice. I helped her. We each took a fine-tooth comb and she was eventually lice free with no awful haircut. "

"Really?"

"Yeah, you don't have to always listen to what the doctor says. I can help if you want!"

"That would be great. There's only one problem."

"What?"

"She's three, which means she can't sit still for more than a minute."

"Well, we need the Trolls movie and whatever her favorite thing to eat is. It'll be fine. You'll see."

Weston smiled at me. He was so incredibly handsome. I stared at him for a little longer than what I should as he backed up his truck and we pulled out of the driveway. I wasn't thinking of liking him, I was just admiring a man that was a provider, a loving dad and hopefully not someone addicted to drugs. He still had all his freckles from when he was a kid, speckled over his nose and cheeks. At a quick glance, you might not even know they were there, but growing up he was teased about them by the other kids. It was common for red heads, but Weston had dark brown hair. I never took part in the teasing because I always admired Weston's looks. He hovered around six feet with a thin frame, but not too thin. It was his smile that always got to me.

"That's the nursing home Sherry's in," Weston said, softly

while he pointed to a brick building with yellow writing. It read The Golden Years.

"The Golden Years. Is that some kind of sick joke?" I chuckled.

"Certainly not a funny one," he replied, looking deep in thought.

"Do you ever visit her?"

"We did this morning. Right Olivia?"

I turned around to watch Olivia respond, but she was far too engrossed in the song to acknowledge her daddy. That is, if she even heard him speaking to her. Gosh did she come alive with music.

My phone began to ring in my lap. It was Travis.

"Are you going to answer that?" Weston asked.

"It's him. I'm not ready yet." The familiar ping signaling there was a voicemail sounded. I swiped the screen on my phone to delete the voicemail.

"Wait," Weston said, abruptly grabbing the phone out of my hands. "Turn off your location before you listen to it."

"I wasn't going to listen to it. I was just going to delete it. Like I said, I'm done. I'm not ever going back to him."

"Well, I turned off your location anyway, just in case he tries to track you down using your cellphone."

"It's in my name, like everything else is. He doesn't even know the usernames and passwords to anything but our checking account."

"Why?"

"Well for one thing, I do the bills and I mean, he wanted it that way. Small business owner trying to protect himself I guess."

"What about your house then?"

"I'll keep making the mortgage payments if that's what you're asking. I would never purposely try to hurt Travis and the last thing I want to do is make him homeless. I still care about him, but he's not the Travis I fell in love with."

Weston just sat there as we drove, listening to my confessions.

"Travis is and has always been my biggest weakness. I guess his would be heroin. It's like, I always give in and go back. I want to believe him, that he can change. That's why I can't listen to that voicemail. Just his voice would have me driving back. I get mad and I hate him and then my heart softens and we're right back where we were. It's been a vicious cycle. I can't imagine you understand what I am telling you. I'm just praying right now I stay strong. I'm young and I know there has to be someone out there that will love me more than heroin."

"I think it gets easier, if you just hang in there. Maybe change your number."

"Yeah, that's a good idea."

I looked behind me and saw Olivia was now sleeping.

"She's out cold Weston. Want to just order some subs and we'll eat back at the house?"

"Okay."

Weston ran into the shop and bought some subs. The silence stretched between us on the ride home. I wanted so desperately to ask about Olivia's mother, but I didn't dare. I knew better than anyone how uncomfortable it felt to be questioned, regardless of how innocent the questions were.

I thought back to our childhood. I always had a little crush on Weston. He was like an older brother to me, only he was much nicer to me than my own. He never made me feel like a tagalong, even though that's exactly what I was. He even gave me his favorite Hawkeye hat. I hung it up on the belt rack in my room and would think of him every time I looked at it.

As time went on, he stopped hanging out with my brother.

He started hanging out with the wrong crowd, had so many absences from school he was suspended for a week and eventually dropped out. Sherri went to wake him one morning and he had runaway. Maura and I stopped hanging out once we got to high school and I just lost touch with their family. There were no hurt feelings, we just went our separate ways.

Olivia woke as soon as Weston parked his truck at the house.

"You hungry?" I asked her. She nodded her head. I got out and unbuckled her and carried her sleepy head into the house, following Weston. He watched me the entire time, but his expression gave nothing away as to what he was thinking.

"Oh, you bought a treat too?" I asked as I watched Weston place ice cream into the freezer.

"Yeah, I ran next door to the convenience store after I ordered the subs. You must not have seen me."

"I was watching Olivia sleep. She is so precious."

"She's my angel," he said, kissing her on the head. It was the closest he had gotten to me all day. His cologne filled my nostrils and it smelled heavenly. I promised myself right then that no matter what, Weston couldn't be my rebound.

"Weston, where's this angel's momma?" I whispered, afraid I was being too bold.

"No longer here," he sighed, turning away from me. He obviously didn't want to talk about it, so I didn't push the matter.

We ate lunch. Weston had ordered me an Italian sub and it was amazing! I set Olivia up with a bowl of ice cream while Weston put Trolls on for her to watch.

"Do you mind if I go mow the lawn while you do this? I just feel weird that I put the For Sale sign up today and the grass needs mowing. I mean, I've seen this movie a thousand times..."

"No...go. We'll be fine. I'll come get you if either of us need anything."

"Perfect, thanks." Weston crouched down low next to Olivia so they were on the same eye level. "Daddy is going to go mow the lawn. I'll be right back." Olivia looked right past Weston, her eyes glued to the television. "Yeah, you won't even notice I left, kid," he said, kissing her on the forehead. We exchanged smiles and he was gone.

I read the box of lice shampoo Weston had bought earlier in the morning. I shampooed her hair and when she was done eating her ice cream, we went to the bathroom to rinse it out. I went to town on Olivia's hair using the nit comb, placing her hair in sections and then starting at the roots. I continuously swooshed the comb in warm water. It was tedious, but the sad look on Weston's face when he talked about cutting Olivia's curls off motivated me to keep going. If this gorgeous hair was the only thing that reminded Weston of Olivia's mother, then I had to do whatever I could to keep it.

"I'll be right back, Olivia. I'm going to go get some fresh water," I said, being ignored by her the same way Weston was. I looked out the window to see Weston pushing a lawnmower. *Ugh, he was so delicious. What was it with guys covered in glass clippings that was such a turn on?* I saw him wave. *Shit*! He totally caught me checking him out. I quickly went to the sink, dumping the water and refilling the bowl. I didn't even wave back. *How rude!*

I continued to comb Olivia's hair. A few moments later I heard the door open.

"Cora..." I heard Weston yell. I got up and made my way to the door.

"Yeah?"

"Oh, hey. You didn't have to get up. I was going to yell to you..."

"What's up?" I asked.

"I'm done mowing. I'm just going to take a quick shower and I'll be right there," he said, wiping the sweat from his brow with his shirt. I caught a sneak peak of his abs. I started counting his six pack...eight pack...

"Cora?"

"Yeah...sure...no problem. I'll just be here...comb, combing away," I said, sounding like a complete idiot. *Comb, combing away? Really? Oh lord, is Weston sexy! I really, really mustn't get distracted right now.*

****

"Still working on her hair, huh?" Weston asked after he emerged from the bathroom. I suddenly felt shy under his watchful gaze.

"Almost finished."

"Well I really appreciate it. I hope you know that." I looked at Weston, smiling warmly. A bead of water dripped down the side of his face, leftover from his shower. I just wanted to lick it right off him. *What was going on with me? Why all of a sudden was I so horny?*

I followed Weston with my eyes as he made his way across the room.

"What are you doing?" I asked him when he started pulling VHS tapes out of the TV stand.

"The realtor tells me I have to clean this place out."

"Why you?"

"Sherri only put my name on the house. None of my siblings. They are a bit bitter, to say the least. I know what you're thinking. Why put it in her stepson's name when she had two kids of her own? I have no idea why. None of us do. If anything, I gave her the most hell growing up."

Olivia kept still as I continued to comb.

"Look it here, Maura and Cora's science project, a home video."

"Oh come on, you have got to be kidding me! Seriously?" I asked in disbelief. The video had to have been twenty years old.

"Oh yeah and when Trolls is over, this is definitely going in."

I cracked up laughing, placing my hand over my eyes in embarrassment. I could remember that school project like it was yesterday. We were studying how things were found inside amber. We filmed at my parents' house. Maura was a tree frog who fell out of the tree into amber. I remember she seriously injured her ankle jumping out of the tree and I cheered her on thinking she had fantastic acting skills. I felt terrible after realizing she was truly hurt.

When I was done with Olivia's hair, I cleaned up the lice contents and bowl of ice cream. I scooped her into my arms and laid her down on the couch. She kept her eyes glued to the television, mesmerized by the movie.

"Hey Weston, would it be weird if I showered quickly?"

"Oh yeah. Sorry, you probably feel gross from the lice. Thank you again for doing that for her. You have no idea how much it means to me."

"No, not at all. It's my pleasure, honestly. I just haven't showered in a couple of days and I'm starting to feel gross," I explained with a nervous laughter. I felt very awkward asking to shower, but I wasn't sure when the opportunity would arise again.

"You know where the bathroom is. Shampoo and stuff is in there."

"Thanks," I said and retrieved to the truck to find my air-dried clothes. I gave them a sniff, relieved to find they smelled just fine. I made my way to the bathroom, grinning to myself that I would shower in the same stall sexy Weston just showered in. He was the last thing I needed right now, but a girl could dream. The warm water cascading over my body instantly made me feel rejuvenated. *Where am I going to go? What am I going to do? Two days sober of Travis. Stay strong, stay strong. I can do this. I'm thirty now, nobody wants me. No, I'm still young! I have my whole life ahead of me.*

When I returned downstairs, Weston was putting a VHS into the player. He had stacked a pile of the ones he wanted to watch. We spent the rest of the afternoon watching home videos. It made me miss the good old days. I watched myself on the television, running across the yard jumping around...not a care in the world back then.

When I looked over, I saw Olivia on Weston. Both were fast asleep. They looked so peaceful. I envied their love for one another. I got up from the couch and tip-toed over to them, carefully taking Olivia into my arms and carried her upstairs to the toddler bed I had seen earlier. She awoke as I placed her down.

"Daddy?"

"Daddy's sleeping. Do you wear a diaper at night?"

Olivia nodded her head yes. She pointed to the dresser. I opened the drawer and sure enough there were diapers in there. I put one on her and covered her with blankets. I rubbed her back until she was asleep again and then I made my way back downstairs.

I felt out of place as I watched Weston sleep, like I was intruding on someone else's family. I knew I should've woken Weston so he could take Olivia home, but the truth was, I didn't want to be alone tonight. Being in their company today felt so refreshing.

I found some blankets in the linen closet by the front door

and placed a blanket over him. I shut off the living room light and used the glow from the television to find my way back to the couch opposite where Weston lay undisturbed. I curled up onto my side and drifted off.

I awoke suddenly to the sound of a phone ringing. I caught a glimpse of Weston jumping off the couch, fumbling to catch his phone before it fell to the floor.

"Shit, it's my first client. I'm late!" he grumbled, looking around. "Where's Olivia?"

"I brought her upstairs."

"SHE HAS NO DIAPER ON!"

"I put one on her last night. She knew where they were...relax!"

"Why didn't you wake me?" he growled.

Because I'm selfish and wanted a place to stay other than my cold lonely camper.

"I don't know, it was getting late. You and Olivia both fell asleep...sorry."

Weston was rambling now and I couldn't make out his words.

"Now I have to wake Olivia," he said, sounding irritated.

"Let her sleep. She's fine here. Come back for her later."

He paused and looked at me, debating on whether or not he could trust me with his most prized possession.

"Weston, Olivia is fine with me. When she wakes up, I'll feed her breakfast, brush her teeth, get her dressed and we'll have fun. I promise! I was a nanny for four years and I love children. She'll be okay!"

"She has no toothbrush here."

"Then I'll take her out and pick one up. Please, it's no big deal."

"Okay. I'll be back as soon as I can."

"Okay."

"Thank you," he said, turning to leave.

"No problem."

"I'll leave the diaper bag by the door."

"Okay."

"The car seat, too."

"Okay, Weston," I mumbled through my sleepy voice.

The truth was, Olivia would be a piece of cake. I nannied for a family of three children, ages three, eighteen months and four months. In fact, I thought children were pretty easy to figure out. You sit with them, give them love and attention and the day will be great. It's adults that complicated things for me.

I laid there thinking about the odd situation I had gotten myself into. I ran away from my husband, slept overnight at my childhood best friend's house, which was five houses away from my parents who I hadn't seen in years. I couldn't give much thought to my next plan in life because I heard a pitter patter of little feet making their way down the stairs. The fear crept across Olivia's face as she searched for Weston and realized he wasn't here.

"Olivia, Daddy is at work, but he will be back soon. Are you hungry?"

Distract her with food.

Olivia just stood there staring at me.

Oh no.

"Do you drink chocolate milk?"

Surely, anything with chocolate in it could win her over. She shook her head yes.

"Okay, let's get dressed and we'll get some chocolate milk for you."

I headed to the door to find the diaper bag Weston said he would leave. Sure enough, it sat by the door, bulging at the seams. I carefully took everything out and displayed it on the floor. Weston had everything you could possibly think of and enough clothes to last a week. Just another cue he was a wonderful father.

I got Olivia dressed and brushed her hair. We made our way to my truck, fastening the car seat into the back and then we were on our way. I slowed down as I passed my parent's house, looking for any sign of life. "They must not be home," I muttered to myself to ease the pang of guilt. *Keep driving*.

I played the Troll's soundtrack over the truck speakers using the Bluetooth on my phone. I watched Olivia's face light up in my rearview mirror. She was beautiful.

I ordered a bagel with vegetable cream cheese, five munchkins, a coffee and a chocolate milk through the drive-thru Dunkin Donuts. I decided to drive to the bike trail in Des Moines. The weather was nice and there were picnic tables at the entrance to the trail. I knew kids loved being outside and I could use the fresh air.

I setup breakfast on an old wooden picnic table and was taken aback when Olivia climbed into my lap to eat. I watched her devour every munchkin and then the entire half of my bagel. I waited until she was content before I ate the rest of the food.

"Did you enjoy that?"

She nodded her head. I was starting to wonder if she would ever talk to me. I threw the rest of the contents into the trash "Let's go for a walk."

We were about five minutes into our walk when Olivia reached up and grabbed my hand. Her skin was so soft. I looked down at her and smiled, grateful for the affection.

"Doggy!" Olivia cried in excitement as a Saint Bernard was heading straight for us. She kept walking towards the dog and stopped abruptly as it licked her face. She was all smiles.

Olivia just spoke!

"I'm so sorry, he loves little kids," the man explained. He was young, medium-height and thin, with straight jet black hair and tan skin. He was wearing aviators that showed my reflection and was quite attractive.

"No problem, as long as he's friendly." It was so nice to hear Olivia talk without her glued to Weston's leg.

"You remind me of my best friend from high school," the man said, smiling at me. "She ran away halfway across the country though."

I lifted my sunglasses from my eyes for a moment, staring at the man. I only had one male best friend in high school.

"Athun, is that you?" I laughed nervously. The man was dressed in medical scrubs.

"Cora! It is you!"

I jumped at Athun, crashing my body against his. If there was one person I missed terribly throughout the last twelve years, it was Athun. We were inseparable in our own little world throughout high school. We were in the same grade, but only began talking once we started working together. I remember the first time I saw him, I was intimidated by him. We didn't hang around with the same group of friends. He was always getting in trouble at school. I had even heard he threw a desk at one of our English teachers. I thought he didn't have anything to offer to my life, but I had never been so wrong.

Athun was the oldest of four boys. He had a temper, but a heart of gold. He lived on the edge, always wore a true smile when he was up to no good. None of my friends understood what I saw in him and many of his friends made fun of me. I was a goody two shoes and popular, but that never stopped us from having a good time. Right before we graduated from high school, he tattooed my name inside a heart on the inside of his arm. I'll never forget the day he showed me, I thought it was fake. I tried desperately to grab his wrist to wash it off, but he insisted I couldn't touch it because it still hurt. It was the most thoughtful gesture anyone had ever done and it made me feel unbelievably cherished.

I grabbed his arm and turned it to get a better look.

"What? Did you think I had it removed?"

"Covered up maybe."

"Why?"

"I ran away, never talked to you again. I don't deserve to be on this arm anymore."

"You were in love."

I stood there with my hand still holding his arm, brushing my thumb over the tattoo.

"Still in love?" he asked.

"Long story."

"I have time."

"I don't. I promised this little one here a walk. Her name is Olivia and I'm just watching her for today." Olivia used my leg as a shield from Athun.

"You live in town now?" he asked.

"No and I'm not sure how long I'll be staying either."

"Here's my number," he said, handing me a business card. "Let's catch up...tonight even."

"Okay, sounds good. I'll text you later." I gave him a hard squeeze. I wasn't much of an affectionate person, but I was beyond happy to see such a wonderful part of my past. It was just what I needed right now, my ride or die friend.

We walked until Olivia grew tired and then I gave her a piggy back ride the entire walk back. I looked for Athun when we returned to the parking lot, but he was already gone. I stopped at the local grocery store on the way back to the house and bought

Olivia a toothbrush, along with two salads for lunch. I picked Olivia up as we made our way around the salad bar. She pointed out everything she liked. Her salad cost fourteen dollars, but I didn't care. I was enjoying every minute of her company.

I turned into Weston's driveway and was met by three police cruisers. They all had their emergency lights flashing. *OH NO!* I felt my heart about to beat out of my chest as I unbuckled and quickly jumped out of the truck.

"IS OLIVIA WITH YOU?" Weston shouted while running towards my truck. The officers followed.

"Of course! Why?"

"Oh, thank God," he said, quickly moving to the side of my truck and opening the back door.

"Ma'am, where did you take this man's daughter?"

"What?" I whipped my head towards Weston who was cradling Olivia in his arms.

"You thought I was trying to kidnap her?" I shrieked.

Weston came around to the front of the truck now.

"You left the door unlocked! You left no note and everything of Olivia's was gone! What did you want me to think?"

"That I'm not the kind of person who would be capable of abducting your little girl! So now you're going to arrest me?" I asked the officer standing next to me. "For going to get her a toothbrush and some lunch? Go ahead, look in the bag there."

"She's okay. It's fine," Weston said.

"We went and bought a toothbrush. I told you that!" It was all I could do not to wind up and punch Weston square in the face.

"I don't have your phone number. I have no way of reaching you!"

"And whose fault is that?" I yelled.

"You had my daughter," he said, his voice cracking.

Holy shit. These feelings of Weston's were VERY real. My heart sunk when his face turned towards the sun and revealed a glisten in his eyes. Right then I realized he was right, I should've left a note.

"We're good here. I overreacted and I've wasted your time. I apologize," Weston told the officers, remaining on the verge of tears. My shoulders slouched in defeat.

"Would you like us to escort her off your property, sir?"

WHAT?

"No, that won't be necessary."

Damn right it won't be! I still have to get my camper and then apparently get out of here.

I watched the officers get into their vehicles to leave. I jumped into my truck and pulled further into the driveway and out of the way. I sat there still in shock, watching the officers drive by. I calmly got out of the truck, grabbing Olivia's diaper bag, car seat and grocery bag. I walked over to the front steps where Olivia and Weston were now sitting. If it weren't for Olivia watching, I think I'd combust into tears.

"I told you I would be right back for her," he said in defense, but I had no energy left to argue.

"I took Olivia for a walk on the bike trail and then we stopped for the toothbrush and some lunch."

"You left the door unlocked," he repeated.

"I didn't have a key to get back in once I left, Weston." I explained, my voice just above a whisper. It didn't matter what Weston said to justify his actions, the damage was already done.

"What took you so long?" he went on. "I told you I would be right back. I knew I shouldn't have let you take her! I called the house multiple times and there was no answer. I come here and the door is unlocked and everything I left you is gone! What am I supposed to think?"

"I am not some kind of monster that could ever harm your daughter. If we took too long, it's because Olivia wanted to stop and pet every dog that walked past her. I'm genuinely sorry. I was only trying to help you today. I think I've overstayed my welcome!"

If I had just left a note none of this would've happened. I took the salad and toothbrush out of the bag and handed them to Olivia. She had a hard time not dropping the heavy container. I handed the diaper bag and car seat to Weston. I knelt in front of Olivia and looked into her caramel colored eyes. "I had so much fun with you today. Thank you." She rewarded me with a smile. "I'll see you around," I said, rubbing the top of her head affectionately. I turned around to leave.

"Did you have fun today?" I heard Weston ask Oliva.

I climbed into my truck in efforts to re-hitch my camper. This would take a few dreaded minutes because honestly, I just wanted to get out of here as fast as possible. I jumped when I heard a knock on my window. Weston was standing on the foot bar of my truck, holding on to my mirror with his head up to the glass. I regretfully put my window down, not wanting to hear anymore.

"I'm so sorry," he breathed. His words were soft and genuine, which brought a thick ball of tears up into my throat. I swallowed down the hurt...something I was very used to doing.

"I am too."

"You are?"

"You know me, but you don't really know me. I mean, if you had just left me your number..."

"I know. I forgot and that was bad parenting on my part. I was just in such a rush this morning. I got to the client's house and he wasn't home. He had left me a voicemail this morning saying something had come up and he needed to reschedule. I should've listened to it. I was frustrated with myself. I turned around and came right back. I waited for so long and I was already pissed off that my imagination ran away and I thought something awful had happened. After Olivia's mother died, it's like I'm so afraid I'll lose Olivia too. I can't go through that again. Olivia is the only part of my life that makes it worth living."

Weston placed his forehead down on my door and closed his eyes. I didn't know what to do.

"I don't think you're a monster," he said.

I was at a loss for words. *What did he want from me? Did he want me to stay?* Deep down I wanted to so I could feel a part of something. Weston opened his eyes and looked at me.

"You were the sweetest kid out of our neighborhood gang. Remember you went through that white rapper stage? You wore those gold fingernails and belly shirts. Oh...and those raps you came up with."

"Please don't remind me! I truly thought I was going to be the first female rapper from the Midwest," I laughed. "I was awful, but I remember thinking I was so good at the time."

"You were!" He was laughing now, too.

"No I wasn't. Everybody made fun of me."

"Maybe your brothers, but I never did. I always looked forward to hearing your latest rap and seeing what you were going to wear. You had some pretty killer outfits!" he teased. "It was adorable."

"Yo...check it out. Without a doubt I must leave, but please don't feel bad for me. Just know, wherever I go I'll be okay. It's just another day of sunshine and play...that's all I really have to say," I chuckled, letting my frustration with Weston dissipate.

"Stay," he said. I turned my face to meet his, wondering if I had heard him correctly. "I don't want you to leave angry. Besides, where will you go? I get that you don't want to see your parents just yet…"

"I'm not angry, Weston. I am hurt, but I will get over it. The last thing I want to do is intrude on your life."

"No, don't think that," he said, reaching inside my truck and turning off the ignition. He pressed the button to release my seatbelt and his hair brushed across my forehead, bringing this warm sensation flooding throughout my entire body.

"I don't know," I said, knowing full well Weston already had it set in his mind I was staying.

"At least eat lunch with us. What the heck did you buy Olivia anyway?" he asked, completely ignoring my hesitation. "I think the container weighs as much as she does."

I laughed.

"Salad. She pointed and I scooped."

"Come on! We'll eat outside. It's nice out."

I grabbed my salad on the front seat and cautiously followed Weston and Olivia to the deck. The truth was, Weston had hit a nerve Travis used to hit all the time. The nerve that made me feel bad about myself, like I was made out to be somebody that I wasn't. I think Weston knew I was upset. I felt his eyes on me the entire time I ate, probably wondering why I wasn't much of a conversationalist like the day before.

"I go play?" Olivia asked when she finished. She had put only a small dent in her salad.

"Sure, the door is open." Olivia hopped down and went inside the house.

"I didn't even know Olivia ate half of that stuff. She loves fruit, but raw vegetables, sunflower seeds and cottage cheese? I hadn't a clue."

I remained silent, begging myself to let it go.

"Are you still mad at me?" Weston asked.

I waited a moment to think about which way I wanted to

approach his answer.

"I have never had anyone call the cops on me before. I am not mad at you. I'm just so incredibly hurt and truthfully, I'm still in shock. I ran away so I could get away from this. Every cop in my town knew me on a first name basis. You hit this place inside my soul just like Travis always did. No matter how hard I tried, I was always in the wrong. Nothing I did was ever good enough. When you feel that way for so long, you start to believe that you're never going to be enough. I thought that by leaving Mass, I was going to get away from feeling that way and then here I am, feeling the same...exact...way. Only this time it's not by some junkie. It's you, someone I looked up to my entire childhood."

I started crying. "Maybe no matter how hard I try to be a good person, it'll just never be enough."

"Please don't say that," Weston whispered into my ear. He was next to my side in an instant with his arm around my shoulder. The contact made me flinch and I prayed Weston didn't notice. I hadn't been touched by another man other than Travis since I was a teenager.

"I'm sorry I'm crying. I feel damaged inside and I'm SO tired of feeling this way."

"I'm a complete asshole. I never meant to make you feel any less than the wonderful person you are. I promise! I learned with Olivia's mother that I have no control in life and that makes me crazy sometimes. I overreacted! She's my whole world, Cora."

"I know."

After a moment of sitting there wondering where this conversation was going to go, Weston spoke.

"I think I know how to cheer you up."

I doubt that...

"You do?"

"Yeah. You clean up lunch and I'll go get Olivia. I'm taking you both somewhere."

"Okay." I wasn't up for a surprise, but I chose to just go along with it. I cleaned up lunch and brought the trash inside. I heard Olivia squeal the entire way up from the basement. *What was she so excited about?* Weston put the car seat into his truck while I grabbed the diaper bag and locked the house. When I returned to the truck to leave, I heard Weston telling Olivia to keep the secret.

"What secret are you hiding Olivia?" I turned and looked at her beaming with enthusiasm. She shook her head no.

"I can tickle it out of you."

"Oh no you don't," Weston said. "Patience. Right Olivia?" She nodded her head.

We pulled into the parking lot of an ice cream shop. If there was any kind of grudge I was still holding with Weston, it had disintegrated now. I was secretly kicking myself at how easily Weston was able to win me over, but ice cream was my favorite.

"Two small twists in a cone with rainbow sprinkles," Weston said, looking at me to order now. "I'm buying," he added.

"Make that three please. I'll have the same," I said.

"Wow, I never pegged you for a soft serve girl. I thought for sure it would be a sundae with extra chocolate, extra whipped cream and a cherry on top." *Was he implying something here?*

"No way, I'm sweet enough. Besides, that's too complex. Colorful on the outside, but simple on the inside."

Just like me.

Weston winked and smiled at me. The eye contact made my heart skip a beat. I wondered what he was thinking as he looked at me.

The ice cream was delicious. I hadn't had soft serve in years.

"Thank you," I told him, trying my best to sound sincere.

"Don't thank me yet."

"Why?"

"The night's not over," he said, pointing behind the ice cream parlor.

I shrugged my shoulders, not able to see what he was talking about.

"Miniature golf. Are you up for it?"

"Yeah, that sounds amazing!" I hadn't played since I lived here. "I didn't even know this place existed back here."

"Just moved to town last summer. I've never been, though."

I took my napkin and wiped Olivia's hands, cleaning her face as well.

"You trying to take my job?" Weston asked.

"No, not at all, sorry. I guess I just enjoy taking care of her."

"I'm teasing. It's nice actually. Sometimes it gets to be a lot playing both parent roles...like I never get a break."

"I can imagine. You make it look easy, though."

"Only to those who are blind."

"Ouch! Did you just call me blind?" I laughed.

We made our way over to mini golf.

"I'll pay this time. I'm starting to feel cheap," I said. Weston handed the clerk a fifty-dollar bill.

"Are you deaf or something?" I teased.

"Yes, tonight I am. I'm deaf and you're blind. What a wonderful combo for mini golfing."

I shook my head. Weston was ridiculous. We grabbed our balls and clubs. I took Olivia on my team, us girls verses Weston. I let Olivia pick our ball. She loved the concept of golf and picked up on it right away. I knew in the back of my mind there was no way we had a chance of winning as I helped Olivia get the ball into the hole, but I didn't care. I was thoroughly enjoying myself. Weston got three holes in one! I had never seen such luck. Olivia and I giggled every time Weston did his happy dance. I think he was enjoying himself just as much as I was.

I thanked Weston again for the wonderful afternoon.

"I should be thanking you," he said.

"For what?"

"You have such patience with Olivia. It's hard to find friends. I mean, none of my friends have kids and then it's hard to go to play activities when I'm trying to run a company. Besides, those single moms are like a pack of wolves. The wedding ring doesn't protect me. When they find out Olivia's mother passed away, they try to swoop right in. It's hard for Olivia to make friends. She hates going to my neighbor's house because it's all boys and she says they're mean to her."

"Why do you bring her there then?"

"Convenience. Olivia is going to be bullied when she goes to school. She ought to learn now how to defend herself."

"Weston, these are supposed to be the best years of her life. These very few years she has from birth until she enters kindergarten are essential! You have to set her up successfully for the rest of her life. If she's not happy there, then she can't go there."

"I'm doing my best by myself!"

I turned around to see Olivia sleeping in her car seat.

"I'll watch her. At least I know I can make her happy. Besides, she makes me revert back to childhood and I could really use that right now."

"How much would I pay you?"

I was surprised he would even consider my suggestion. Just hours earlier he thought I was permanently running off with his child.

"I don't want your money."

"Then stay here, in Sherri's house."

"Until it sells?"

"I'll take it off the market."

"I thought the nursing home needs to liquidate Sherri's assets?"

"They do."

"I'll buy the house. How much is it?" I asked.

"How much do you have?"

"That's not an answer. How much did the realtor list this house for?"

"One hundred forty-seven." I just looked at Weston laughing.

"What is so funny about one hundred and forty-seven thousand dollars?"

"This would go for double in Massachusetts, maybe even close to triple."

"So, you can afford that? You'll never get financing without a job."

"I'll buy it with cash. We'll just need a lawyer."

"You have that much money? How?"

"Is that even relevant?"

"Yes, if I'm letting you watch my daughter. How do I know you didn't steal all your husband's money and leave?"

I sat there astounded by his presumptions.

"If you want to know the truth…when I left here, I put myself through college working three jobs. When I graduated, I started working for the college I attended. I worked my way to the top. I was the head of the accounting department and bringing in six figures since I was twenty-three. I was the youngest one in my entire department. I carried me and Travis, bought us our house, our vehicles and the camper. Travis blew anything he made on drugs. That's why seven years ago I started depositing money into my secret savings account. It's none of your business where my money comes from and don't use Olivia to dig for information. I earned every dollar I have."

"Woah. It most certainly is my business where it came from. How do I know you aren't some drug dealer? What kind of father would I be if I just let you into my daughter's life, no questions asked?"

Okay, maybe he does have a point here.

"You know what the best part is?" I asked, ignoring his questions. "Travis blamed my income on why he reverted to heroin. I made more money, so it made him feel less of a man. I guess my money makes you feel insecure, too."

"Okay, okay," Weston said with his hands up in defense.

I was being nasty and I knew it. I so badly wanted to go back to that girl in the home video, the one Weston remembered. She must be in here somewhere. I just had to find her, because I hated who I was now. I jumped out of the truck, careful not to wake Olivia as I shut my door. Weston hopped out too.

"Now just stop! Here I go making you mad again when I'm not even trying to."

"What is the problem with me? WHAT IS IT? I'm not trying to do you any harm, but you keep making me feel like I am!"

"I just don't want to let you into my life and find out you stole from your husband and cops come looking for you. They find you and arrest you and then what? What do I tell Olivia?"

"Is that the truth?"

"Yes, of course it is! I don't know you Cora. I knew you as a kid, but I know nothing about you now."

"What's it going to take?"

"It's not you, it's me. That little girl already has a strike against her and it's my duty as a father to protect her. Okay?"

I nodded my head.

"Am I making you feel like he did?"

"Yes, actually you are. Money was a big deal to him. I don't care about money. I don't know why I hid it in a savings account. Burn it all...donate it...I don't give a shit anymore."

"You don't mean that. You put that money aside to start a new life and that's exactly what you're doing. Don't buy this house. I will figure something out. You don't want to make any permanent decisions right now."

"Yes, I do. It's right down the street from my parents and they're getting older. I'll need to take care of them soon."

Ugh! My parents. I must go see them soon.

"I'll bide you some time for you to think about it, okay?"

"Okay."

I opened the door for Weston as he brought Olivia inside and upstairs to her room sound asleep. I sat at the kitchen island, waiting for him to return.

"I think this is yours," he said, handing me a card. I read it, Athun Lom, OB/GYN. I started laughing.

"What's so funny? It's yours, isn't it?"

"Yes, I ran into him today on the bike trail."

"And he wants to give you an exam?"

I started laughing really hard. The confusion on Weston's face furthered my laughter.

"I had no idea he was an obstetrician-gynecologist. He was my best friend in high school."

"I thought my sister was your best friend."

"We parted ways when we got to ninth grade, said hi to each other in the hall, but I didn't like the people she hung out with. Anyway, Athun was always a tough guy, so it's hard to believe he's in this field now."

"Why?"

"He's a guy, so he doesn't even have a vagina. That's like a priest lecturing a couple on marriage. He has no idea what he's saying because he's never been married."

"There's nothing wrong with a male gynecologist. I think it's great actually."

"Of course you would." Weston chuckled.

"So this guy, he wants to catch up or something?"

"Yeah, wants to go to dinner tonight."

"Are you going to go?"

"I don't know...I have nothing to wear. I only brought what I could hold in my two hands."

"Wow. You don't own any material possessions?"

"I find they don't keep you warm at night," I replied.

"A blanket does."

I shook my head at him grinning. "You know what I mean."

"I know, I'm teasing. Sherri's closet is full of dresses, if you want to take a look."

"You don't think that's a little weird?"

"No. Women overthink things! If you were in a nursing home and couldn't wear your nice clothes, wouldn't you want someone else to get some use out of them?"

I thought about that for a moment.

"Yeah, I guess."

Weston pointed to Sherri's room.

"I remember," I said, wandering through the door and stopping in front of her closet. I guess taking a peek wouldn't hurt. I switched the light on and peered inside. I ran my fingers down all the dresses. There had to be at least fifty. Sherri was always immaculately dressed from head to toe, like she belonged on the cover of a magazine. I found a few dresses right away that were beautiful. I dropped to my knees, picking a shoe at random to see if we were the same size. A little small, but they would do. I found two pairs that were most comfortable and returned to the kitchen to find Weston on the phone. I dropped the contents onto the washer machine and stepped outside to phone Athun.

"Athun," I heard after the third ring.

"Hi, it's Cora."

"Hey! I was wondering if I would hear from you."

"Yeah, just seeing if I could take you up on that dinner offer."

"Great! I just bought a new house. Do you want to come check it out? We could order some food and catch up."

"Sure."

"I'll text you my address...say five o'clock?"

"Perfect! See you soon."

I hung up looking at my watch. It was almost three. I went back inside to find Weston finishing his phone call.

"You find anything nice?" he asked.

"Yes, but it was useless because he wants to stay in and catch up."

"That only means one thing."

"Yes, I'll be overdressed wearing any of Sherri's clothes."

"No, it means he wants you in his bed," Weston said, smirking.

"It does not! Our friendship was never like that. He always told me I was too skinny and he liked girls with a little meat on their bones."

"You're naive."

"Well, he does have a tattoo of my initials."

"WHAT?"

"Yeah, inside a heart with two birds."

Weston looked at me like I was a complete idiot.

"The tattoo signified our friendship."

"Whatever you say..."

"I'll ask him tonight then. I'll bet you one hundred bucks you're wrong."

"Deal." We shook hands. The contact sent shivers running up my spine.

Bad...very bad.

"I better go take a shower," I said, heading outside to the truck and grabbing an outfit consisting of jeans and a sweatshirt. I was running low on socks and underwear. I would definitely have to go shopping soon.

I was quite excited as I showered, thinking about seeing Athun again. I was hoping he hadn't changed much. He was perfect! I checked myself out in the mirror before I left the bathroom. I looked happy. I was happy. Homeless and happy.

"Hey Weston."

"Yeah?"

"Could I do some laundry?"

"Cora?"

"Yes?"

"You do whatever you want. I told you, it's yours. Fill the fridge with food, wash your clothes and help me out with Olivia while I work, okay?"

"For how long?" I asked.

"Until you want to go."

"Okay."

"You don't like my idea?" he asked.

It was my idea.

"I do...very much so. It's perfect!"

There's that smile again and it's melting my heart. I grabbed the dresses and shoes from the washer machine to return them to Sherri's closet.

"Leave them," Weston said. "Olivia and I will take you out another night. I know just the restaurant!"

"Okay, I better go. Will I see you when I get back?"

"I don't know. If not, I'll leave you my key under the mat."

"Okay."

"Enjoy tonight. Maybe he could teach you a thing or two about your vagina," he teased.

"Seriously? Did you really just say that?"

I heard him cracking up as I closed the door behind me. I punched Athun's address into my GPS. I had a half hour to spare so I stopped by the mall on the way to pick up some socks and underwear. I was almost out of cash from my wallet and would need to set up a checking account soon.

I found Athun's address without any issues. His house was beautiful. There was a lot of stone work on the front with white pillars. *Fancy*. I pegged Athun for a maintenance man or retail clerk, something that didn't involve schooling. I was still blown away that he was a doctor.

"Hey," he said after he swung the door open and saw me standing there on his front step. I suddenly felt shy.

"Hey! Your house is amazing, Athun," I said, wrapping my arms around his waist. It felt so nice to be in Athun's embrace again.

"Thank you. I'm still getting used to the place. I love it, though. Come on in!"

The entryway had cathedral ceilings with an open staircase to the top.

"I'll give you a tour."

Athun took me around the house. *What would a single guy want with a four-bedroom and three bath house?*

"So, do you have any children?" I asked.

"Gosh no! You would need a woman for that."

"No takers, huh?"

"No, I think it's the whole obstetrician-gynecologist thing."

"Well I have to admit, I was a bit taken aback when I read your business card. I even looked you up online thinking it was a joke. I mean, why?"

"Why not?"

"Well, first of all, you don't have a vagina. How are you going to educate me on equipment you don't even own?"

"Four years for a bachelor's degree, another four for my medical degree and a four-year residency. That's how."

"Exactly my point, Athun! You hated school!"

"I bet I know more about your vagina than you do," he said, trying to change the subject.

"Well, we won't test that knowledge...not tonight anyway," I said, smirking. Athun was amused too. "Come on. What gives? All you ever did was talk down on the idea of college. You even called me a yuppie for wanting to go! I get it, you're a young heterosexual guy, but the vagina isn't all that pretty, especially after having children."

"I'm not in this field for a living so I can look at the female anatomy every day. After you left, my mom got uterine cancer. I guess it just brought out this calling in me I never knew existed. My family had the same reaction you're having right now, but I don't think of it as a sexual thing. I don't get aroused when I examine a woman. I feel like I am helping her."

"I'm so sorry about your mom. I had no idea. I guess when you put it that way, that it touches you on a personal level, I can understand. But I could also see how it would make a woman feel...insecure."

"Insecure?"

"Certainly. If you're examining breasts and vagina every day, seeing what other women look like, then you may be comparing your significant other to them."

"For the record, I have never actually done that."

"Sure you have. You have never had a girl in your bed and thought, *that is one good looking vagina*?"

"I'm going to need a beer if we are going to keep having this conversation."

I started laughing. Athun took two beers out of the fridge and cracked them open.

"I should probably eat something first. You know how one beer goes right to my head."

"Still?" he asked, surprised. "Good to know, though. It'll get you to open right up," he said, grabbing some burgers from the refrigerator. "Instead of takeout, I think I'll spark up my new grill. Are you okay with that?"

"Perfect!"

I watched him grab some vegetables out of the fridge and then move about the kitchen grabbing skewers, a cutting board and a knife.

"I'll do this, you tend to your meat," I said.

"Was that supposed to be some kind of anatomy joke?"

"Not at all, but thanks a lot for making me feel awkward now."

"Cora...you, awkward?"

"No, I'm teasing you. I have never felt awkward in your presence."

I began chopping vegetables and putting them on the skewer. Athun maneuvered around me grabbing burger fixings and preparing cheeseburgers. He opened the sliding glass door and stepped outside. When I was finished with the skewers, I went to find him.

"Wow, you have a pool and a hot tub. It's a dream out here!"

"Yeah, I completely forgot to tell you to bring your suit."

"I don't currently own one. Well I do, but they're over a

thousand miles away and I'm never going back."

"Are you divorced?"

"No."

"Did you run away?"

I nodded my head.

"Cora! That's never going to fix things."

"Apparently you can't fix someone addicted to heroin."

"Travis? Heroin?"

I nodded my head again.

"Wow, I never would've thought. I mean, I didn't like Travis much when you introduced us, but that's because you gave all your attention to him. He was a pretty talented musician, though. What does he do now?"

"Had a landscaping business. He did very well the first few years and then I don't know what happened. Maybe he was doing drugs then and I just didn't catch on, but he stopped turning a profit and hasn't for years now."

"So, you carried the both of you?"

"Oh yeah, for quite some time now. It never bothered me. I loved my job, loved making more money than I knew what to do with, but when I found out he was spending that money on drugs, it really got to me."

"Yeah?"

"Yeah. I know some day I will have to deal with it, but I don't even want to think about a divorce right now. The word divorce just makes me feel like a failure. I haven't told my parents; can you imagine their reaction when I drop that bomb on them? They've always thought I was so put together. I'm hiding out for now, trying to see if I can find a little happiness somewhere before I see them again."

"Wow. You've come back home and they don't even know? That shocks me. I mean, of course you can find happiness and you will. I think you'll be surprised at how understanding your parents will be. The love a mother and father feel for their child is unconditional."

"How do you know?"

"I see it all the time when I deliver a baby. That look in the mother and father's eyes when I introduce them to their newborn, sometimes I still hold back the tears. Even when the baby is born with a birth defect, that look their parent gives is just the same, full of love and admiration. This world is cruel at times and I get to be a part of something so beautiful. It's extraordinary."

"Wow."

"Yeah."

We ate dinner by candlelight on Athun's patio. It was wonderful. The food was perfect. When it was time for me to think about leaving, Athun invited me into his hot tub.

"Just go in your bra and underwear. It's the same thing as a bathing suit."

"I can't do that because I know it's really my bra and underwear."

"It's just me. I've seen you naked!"

"That was one breast you saw and I really thought something was wrong with my nipple! It was twice the size as my other one."

"You just got bit by something at the lake that night. So, you aren't going to be any fun tonight?"

Athun removed the cover to the hot tub and tempted me with the steam pouring off the water. It did look rather relaxing.

"Oh Athun, when you put it that way," I said, quickly taking off my clothes and throwing them onto the chair. I scurried into the hot tub.

"Are you serious right now? What are you so ashamed

of?"

"Says the one guy who told me I was too skinny and needed to gain weight. I have always been insecure about my body around you."

"Really?" he asked, like I had just punched him in his gut.

"No, I didn't mean it like that. I've always felt insecure in a bathing suit around anybody."

Athun threw his shirt off along with his shorts, revealing swimming trunks and climbed right in. I couldn't help but stare at his body which was the same from high school, lean, but muscular and chiseled out in all the right places.

"I guess you were prepared," I teased.

"Always am."

I laid my head back and looked up at the stars.

"I think you are beautiful Cora and I am not just saying that. In fact, I think you're more beautiful now than the last day I saw you all those years ago."

"You mean that?"

"Yes, with all my heart. I remember the first time I saw you, we had chemistry class together, but I was too shy to say hi. Then when we started working together and I was kind of forced to grow some balls and talk to you. I thought you were going to be stuck up and not want to talk, but I was very wrong about you. You were my favorite person in high school."

"Clearly," I said, motioning to the tattoo on his arm.

"Every girl I have ever dated has had a problem with this tattoo."

"Really?"

"Oh yeah, it's like my sign. I find a great girl, we start dating and I think she could be the one. Then, out of nowhere she asks if I ever think about having these initials removed. It's right then I realize, she's insecure and it's not going to work. Like I said, it's my sign."

"Every girl?"

"Never fails...every time."

"Wow. So, why not just get it removed?"

"This is my favorite tattoo I have."

"Why?"

"It signifies an array of emotions for me. You didn't belong in my clique, you were the straight A girl and I was a C at best. I had anger issues so uncontrollable that I had to take medicine for it. Do you remember?"

"Yes. I remember finding the prescription in your room when you went to the bathroom. I was googling the name of the medicine when you returned."

"You were my medicine. I stopped taking it after we started hanging out. You taught me how to relax."

"I did?"

"Definitely."

"How?"

"I don't know. I can't explain it, but I wasn't angry about everything in life anymore."

"On our graduation day, your mom told me you lost your voice screaming for me as I walked across the stage to receive my diploma. She told me you loved me and thanked me. I didn't really understand why she was so happy about our friendship."

"You changed me and she saw that."

"Really?"

"Oh yeah. I smoked weed, drank after school and would come home drunk or high as a kite...sometimes even both. I never did any of my homework and was about to fail."

What! I never knew any of this.

"Athun, are you telling me the truth right now?"

"Yes. After you, I stopped the drugs, the alcohol and

started doing my homework. I'll never forget my mom cried on the day she received my report card. I didn't have one letter other than an A or B and all thanks to you."

"Wow," I said, trying to hold back the tears. I could feel my eyes start to glisten and hoped Athun couldn't tell. If there was one person who always knew how to make me feel special, it was Athun.

"I had no idea."

"I tattooed your name on my arm! I mean, c'mon..."

"Everyone told me you did that because you loved me."

"I did...I still do," he said, shrugging his shoulders.

"No, like romantic love, not just a friendship kind."

"I did love you like that. I mean, if you had confessed your love for me, I would've acted on it in a heartbeat."

"Really? Why did you never say?"

"You didn't look at me like that. If I had told you the way I felt, our friendship would have been over. It wasn't worth it to me."

"What about those girls you dated? I was always too skinny and they certainly had that extra cushion for the pushing."

"Yeah, I liked a girl I could hold onto and not feel their bones," he said laughing. "I didn't love you any less because your hips dug into me when I gave you a hug."

"Shut up," I said, playfully splashing water at him.

"You were the first girl I ever loved, which is another reason why I keep your initials inside this heart. It reminds me not to judge someone just by looking at them."

I stared at him staring back at me. I had never thought of Athun as more than anything but a friend. Now, as I looked at him, I wondered if we could ever be romantically involved. The thought was foreign.

"What are you thinking about?" he asked.

"How much I missed you."

"Yeah right! You had Travis so you never thought of me."

"All the time. You were my best friend, Athun! I saw you every day for almost four years. We did everything together!"

"Until you met Travis. I knew he was the one for you. It was like you were mesmerized by him. I just never saw you up and leaving without so much as a goodbye."

"How'd you know?"

"You always had boyfriends here and there, you never stopped hanging out with me, though. I knew our friendship bothered Travis and you chose him over me. If you could toss your best friend aside like that, then I knew it was because he was it for you."

"I did choose him over you and I'm sorry for that. He was just so jealous of you! In retrospect, that should've been a clear indication not to marry him. Instead, he was moving far away and a fresh start sounded nice. I wish I had stayed in touch with you."

"Me too."

I sat there for a moment looking up at the night's sky again.

"Well I better get going. I'm watching that little girl again tomorrow and she's up at the crack of dawn."

"Okay."

"Are you staying in?" I asked.

"Yeah, unless you want me to walk you out."

"No, stay," I said, standing up. "This is me," I said, turning around so he could see my whole body. "I am the kind of skinny super models get paid a lot of money for! Would you like a hip digging hug before I go?"

Athun stood up and grabbed me, practically squeezing the air out of my lungs.

"I thought you'd never ask," he replied, resting his thumbs

over my hip bones. The skin to skin contact sent this euphoric tingling sensation throughout my body. I tried my best to ignore it.

"Am I hurting you?" I teased, pressing my hips into him. "You big baby!"

He remained silent as we stood there for a moment in a warm embrace. I wondered what he was thinking as he held me. When he let go, I just looked up at him. He had this look about him like he was deep in thought. I even wondered if he was going to bend down and kiss me. I held my breath.

"Don't be a stranger," he said.

"I most certainly won't," I exhaled.

I thought about Athun the entire ride home and the fact that he did love me romantically. *Did he still? Could I see myself with him? Who was I kidding? I'm still married.* I took my wedding ring off my finger and tossed it into the center console. It meant nothing to me now.

When I arrived home, Weston's truck was still in the driveway. I found him asleep on the couch. I decided to wake him up. I was wide awake and felt like talking.

"Hey," I said, quietly.

"Hey. What time is it?" Weston asked, blinking his eyes a few times. My stomach fluttered when he smiled at me.

"Eight-thirty...not too late."

"I put Olivia down an hour ago and must have fallen asleep. I figured I would just leave her here so I wouldn't have to drop her off in the morning."

"Okay, that's fine."

"How'd tonight go? Was I right?"

"He didn't try any moves. I told you he wouldn't, but you were kind of right also. The tattoo signifies friendship, but he was in love with me at the time."

"I told you! Pay up!"

"I'm saying fifty bucks because he never actually confessed his love for me."

"Doesn't mean he didn't feel it. He wanted you, so a hundred bucks it is!"

"Fine, I'll give you the money tomorrow. I have to go set up a checking account anyway. I'll take out the money then."

"I'm kidding. Keep the money! I don't need it."

"Oh no! A bet is a bet and you won. I just can't believe he was in love with me! I honestly never thought..."

"Girl, you are so blind."

"Ah, call me that again!"

"What?"

"Girl. In Massachusetts I felt so grown up, like I was old and my life was passing me by. Here, I feel like a kid again. It's like I'm starting with a blank canvas and now I know how I want to paint it."

"Tell me about this art. What do you want to paint?" he asked, sitting up.

He watched me, with what seemed like a bit of apprehension, as I thought about my answer. I know he was curious, but perhaps more unsure as to how I would respond.

"Definitely a house, but a small one...nothing fancy. I'll paint a boat on there because someday I want a boat to go out on the lake. I'll paint a fishing rod and a fish because it was my favorite pastime and I cannot remember the last time I have gone. I'll paint a few friends...I hope to meet a few people I could let into my life. It's hard to let anyone in since I don't want to be judged. Oh, and I'll paint my family of course...if I ever get the courage to face them again."

"Sounds like a masterpiece."

"Really?"

"Yes and you'll get there. I know you will."

"Thanks. So are you leaving right now or staying?"

"Leaving."

I tapped my foot on the floor nervously.

"Stay?" I asked.

"Yeah?"

"Yeah. I feel safe when you're here, which helps me sleep."

"There's an alarm you can set. I have the pin in my wallet. I'll get it for you in the morning. Regardless, you are perfectly safe here. This neighborhood has never had a problem."

"Okay."

"I'll stay, though. I like the cramp in my neck the next day."

"No, I'm being selfish. You have a nice cozy bed at home. Go!"

"A cozy bed is not at all appealing when there is no one to share it with."

Weston kicked off his shoes, turned down the lights until there was just a glow and threw me a blanket. We laid down on opposite couches and looked at each other, not saying a word for a few minutes.

"What are you thinking about, Weston?"

"How I haven't brushed my teeth. My dentist would not be happy."

"You're such a geek!"

"I'm thinking about how simple you appear to be, but how complex I think you truly are," he said.

"Complex how?"

"Inside your heart."

"I think I could say the exact same thing about you."

"Yeah? Do you want to go there tonight?" Weston asked.

"Do you?"

"No. I have a crazy day tomorrow, but I'll take a rain check."

"Rain check it is! Goodnight."

"'Night."

Weston closed his eyes and rolled over. I laid awake running through today's events in my head. Weston thought I had kidnapped his child and now he's letting me watch her AND he's sleeping over, yet again. Life was weird, but I enjoyed not knowing where each day would take me. Before, it was eight to four-thirty working Monday through Friday and I appreciated my routine. I never even gave it a second thought. Now, I wouldn't go back to that lifestyle for a million dollars. The thought of that repetition made my head spin. The same thing every day; I just couldn't do it. I had to find something to do to make money, but at the moment, I wasn't sure I would ever return to accounting. The cubicle life...well, maybe it wasn't for me anymore.

I sat up looking for Weston's phone. I grabbed it off the coffee table and punched my number into his contacts, sending a text message to my phone. I saved my name as "Complex Girl," under his contact list. I quietly placed it back on the coffee table. *Now I have his number.*

CHAPTER FIVE

I woke to Weston's alarm, feeling rather refreshed.

"How's your neck?" I whispered.

"I am so old," he said. "I used to sleep on a couch no problem. I cannot do that again."

He stretched his neck while I stretched my arms up over my head.

"You ever wear pajamas?" he asked.

"I don't have any. I'll go shopping today."

He let out a laugh. "I was just asking. Don't go on my behalf."

"I'd make you coffee and breakfast, but I need to grocery shop too."

"No worries. I stop every morning on my way anyway. I better get going."

"Enjoy your day," I said.

"Olivia and I will take you to dinner tonight, so be ready. I'll come pick you girls up at say, five o'clock?"

"Sure."

"See you later then. I'll leave the car seat by the door again."

"Okay, 'bye."

I laid back down, throwing the blankets over me and falling asleep until I heard Olivia coming down the stairs. Her curls were flopping carelessly about on her head. I grabbed her and swooped her in next to me underneath my blanket. She seemed foreign to affection and I wondered how often Weston hugged her.

"What should we do today?"

"Bagel."

"Yeah? You want another chocolate milk and bagel with vegetable cream cheese?"

She nodded her head.

"I have to shampoo your hair again like yesterday morning and then we will get dressed and leave. Okay?"

She nodded. I looked through her hair and was confident she no longer had lice, but I gave her another shampoo treatment for good measure. After we got ready, I snapped a picture of her smiling and sent it to Weston with a caption underneath that read, "'morning Daddy."

He texted back right away, remarking about how much she looked like her mother. I wondered how painful that must be to see a resemblance of your lost loved one every single day. I didn't text back. We got breakfast and then went to the bank to set up my checking account. The savings account was still in my maiden name and if it wasn't for knowing the bank manager from high school, I would've had some trouble. The look on his face when he saw the balance, I had almost four hundred and fifty thousand dollars. I think my facial expression matched his. In that moment, I felt tremendously proud of myself.

We went to the mall and I bought myself several outfits and pajamas. I even bought Olivia a dress and some shoes for tonight's dinner. We went grocery shopping after, then went home to eat lunch.

"Olivia, I am having a wonderful day with you today." I looked at her smiling. She knew just what I was telling her.

"What would you like to do now?"

"See doggies."

"Okay, we can go to the bike trail again."

We hopped back into the truck and drove down the street to the trail. We were stopped on the side, sitting in a patch of grass, when I heard the familiar voice of Athun.

"Don't you have a job?" I asked, smirking.

"I come here every day to walk Moose, usually after my lunch, unless it's my day off or I'm delivering a baby. What's your excuse?"

"Olivia wanted to come back here today. She loved seeing all the dogs yesterday."

We both turned our attention to Olivia patting Moose on the head.

"He's so big," she commented. She just said three words to me. I was so happy! I snapped a picture of her petting Moose and sent it to Weston, typing out "I know what Olivia wants for Christmas this year."

"So, you have any plans for tonight?" Athun asked.

"Actually, I do. This little girl and her daddy are taking me to dinner."

"That sounds great. Are you two a thing or something?"

"Oh no. I just watch his daughter."

"How'd you land that job? Did you answer an ad or something?"

"No, my best friend Maura from childhood, he's her older brother."

I could tell Athun was hungry for more information, but I didn't feel like going through the play by play.

"Later this week then?" he asked.

"Definitely," I replied, smiling.

I watched Athun tug on Moose's leash. "'Bye Olivia," he said.

"'Bye Moose," she cheered, waving to the dog.

"What do you say we head home? You should take a nap and then we have to get pretty for Daddy! He's taking us out to dinner later. You can wear your new dress and shoes."

Olivia's eyes lit up. She grabbed my hand and we began walking in the opposite direction of Athun, back towards the truck. I think she was finally warming up to me.

"What's your favorite color?" I asked.

"I don't know."

"What about the ABC's? Do you sing them?"

She shook her head.

When we arrived home, I noticed the For Sale sign was gone. I instantly wondered how Weston had negotiated that one. I brought Olivia inside, took her shoes off and carried her up to her bed.

"Stay," she pleaded, holding onto my shirt. I felt the warmth swoosh through my heart, her words mirroring those I said to her daddy just last night. I wondered if mine had the same effect on him as Olivia's did to me. I squeezed in next to her.

"Can I sing you a song?" I asked.

"Yes."

I sang her the A-B-C song and she loved it.

"Have you heard that song before?"

"Ah, I don't know."

"Okay. Well, starting today, every time you go to sleep, we will sing it."

I held her and watched her fall asleep. She was so precious. I knew I would miss her when it was time for me to go. I searched the web on my phone for three-year milestones while she slept. Olivia should know her numbers, colors and the alphabet along with an entire list compiled of physical milestones. I would surely test Olivia on her knowledge when she woke up. I wondered what she did at the babysitter's house all day.

I awoke to the feeling of someone's presence. I sat up, careful not to disturb Olivia and caught sight of Weston in the doorway. I carefully made my way out of the bed and over to where he stood. I walked past him rubbing my eyes.

"Sleep much?" he whispered.

"See why you can't pay me? I'd be making money snuggling."

"That's a good job right there and besides, I bet Olivia thoroughly enjoys it."

"I cannot believe I fell asleep. I haven't napped in years. I'm so groggy."

We made our way downstairs. I tossed the toothbrush I had bought earlier in the day at him. "Here. I don't want your dentist to be angry with you," I said, amused.

"What's this supposed to mean? I can't sleep on that couch again."

"I know. I mean, you've slept here twice before now. I guess I got it for just in case. What time is it anyway? Am I late?"

"No, it's almost four. I'm early."

"Okay, I'm going to go get ready."

I made my way back upstairs to shower. When I go out, I realized I left my clothes downstairs. I wrapped the towel around my body and tiptoed downstairs. I gave Weston an awkward smirk when I saw him sitting on the couch with his phone. As I passed by him again to head upstairs, his voice startled me.

"You might as well change in Sherri's room. She's not ever coming back home."

"That bad, huh?"

"She doesn't even remember who I am. I mean, she has good days and bad. Her long-term memory is better than her short."

"No chance she will ever come back here?"

"No, they started her on medicine and honestly, I don't see a change at all."

"That's so sad. I'm sorry."

"I feel bad for Olivia. She spent a lot of time here. That's why she has a bed, diapers and some clothes. Sherri loved to dote on her."

I stood there listening until I realized I was still in my towel. Excusing myself, I headed to the room and changed, applying minimal makeup and blow drying my hair. When I stepped out, the look on Weston's face was priceless.

"Damn girl! Are you trying to give me a heart attack?"

"Oh hush!"

"I've never seen you look so..."

"Sophisticated?"

"I was going to go for gorgeous. Give yourself some credit!"

I looked down, feeling shy from his compliment.

"Hey Weston, do you think maybe I could move some of Sherri's things aside, that I wouldn't be using?" I mean, if I was going to be a live-in nanny, I felt like I needed my own headquarters.

"Sure. Like what?"

"Well, you tell me to use her room as if it is my own. I would just like to put my clothes in the drawers and maybe put anything I don't want into the basement?"

"Of course. You don't have to ask me that. Donate anything you don't want. That's what I was supposed to do anyway. The realtor told me to, in order to get the house ready to sell."

"Yeah, I noticed the For Sale sign was gone. No more realtor, huh?"

"I didn't notice. He must have come to get it."

"Look, I don't want to get you in trouble with the assisted living place. I can find somewhere else to live."

"I bought it," he blurted out.

"You bought it, it meaning this house?"

"Yes."

"You bought it or you are thinking about buying it?"

"I bought it today. I went to the lawyer's office this morning to sign paperwork. It's a done deal."

"So I couldn't buy it, but you could?" I asked, confused.

"Yeah, I don't know what came over me. I don't know if it's because I don't have time to clean it out or maybe I just want to be able to come here whenever I want. Maybe deep down it's because I want to make sure you have a place to stay and are okay or all of the above."

Unbelievable!

"I'm thirty, not thirteen," I snickered.

"I know, I know."

"I wasn't even a thought inside your mind up until a few days ago and you make a major decision like buying a house just to know I'm okay?"

"It sounds ridiculous, I know. Like I said, something just came over me that told me I had to buy it. Are you mad?"

"I don't know."

"If you decide this is where you want your fresh start, I'll just sell it to you. I promise."

I knew the only way to buy a house that quickly was if you had the cash in full.

"So you paid cash? You have that kind of money?"

"Does *that* bother you?"

"Not at all. What is it you do anyway?"

"My mother sold me her company. I own it with my sister."

"Which sister? You have four."

"Carolyn."

"The chimney sweeping business?"

"Yes."

Just then Olivia appeared in the doorway. She ran and gave Weston a hug.

"I shampooed her hair again today and then looked it over with a magnifying glass. I don't see any lice or their eggs. I think it's safe to say they're gone."

"You're a saint."

"I can't say the same about you."

"Ouch! Can we talk about it later?"

"Certainly. Olivia has a beautiful dress she would like to wear for you tonight."

I grabbed Olivia's hand and our bag of belongings. We got ready and were back downstairs in the matter of minutes.

"What a lucky guy I am tonight. You look beautiful, Olivia," Weston said, giving her a kiss on the cheek.

"Her too," Olivia said, pointing up to me. I was just about to tell Olivia no when Weston leaned in and kissed my cheek. My heart began thumping and my knees became weak. I tried desperately not to show the affect Weston had on me. I smiled shyly. *It was just the cheek for goodness sake.*

"Shall we?" Weston asked.

"Are you going to change too?"

"We'll stop at my house on the way since the restaurant is just down the street."

"Did you already put her car seat in your truck?"

"I stopped and got another one today," he replied.

"Well weren't you just a busy guy today, buying a house and a car seat. What's next?"

"Dinner."

I shook my head at him.

****

Weston's house was perfect. It had a wraparound farmer's porch and cedar clapboard with a red tin roof. It wasn't elegant, nor did it scream "look at me" like Athun's did. It was simple, yet beautiful; exactly the house I'd picture him finding.

"Would you like to come in?" Weston asked while shifting his truck into park.

Now more than ever I felt like I was intruding on someone else's life. I didn't want to go inside and see pictures of his deceased wife scattered along the walls. I would feel heartbroken and tonight, I just wanted a good night.

"That's okay, we'll wait in here."

"Okay, I'll be right back."

We waited for a few minutes and then Olivia grew antsy.

"Can we get out? I want to play." I counted how many words were in those two sentences. Olivia was right on track with her speech.

"Sure! Do you want to play in the front yard?"

"Yeah."

I got out and unbuckled Olivia. She ran into the grass to fetch a ball. When I stepped into the grass, my heels dug into the dirt so I tossed them towards the driveway.

"Kick it here," I told Olivia.

She wound up and kicked the ball, only it went nowhere in my direction. I ran and got it. "Can you catch? Here, hold out your arms like this," I said, showing her how to catch a ball. I threw the ball to her and she caught it first try. I clapped my hands in excitement. She would kick me the ball and I would throw it back to her. This went on for a few minutes until I saw a movement out of the corner of my eye.

"What are you doing?" I asked when I saw Weston sitting on the front steps. His look of admiration sang right to my soul.

"Watching you two."

"Well come on already. I'm starving!"

"It's not every day I get to see two beautiful girls running around my front lawn."

"Especially ones dressed up so fancy," I added.

"Yes. You read my thought exactly."

"Olivia, are you ready?" Olivia ran to the truck. I slipped my shoes back on and ran after her.

"Potty," Olivia told me as I buckled her in.

"You have to go potty?" I asked her and she smiled. "Oh, silly Olivia. Let's go potty inside your house before we go."

I put her back down, setting her on her feet. I watched her find Weston, who walked with her to the front door to unlock it again. I was surprised when he didn't go inside with her, but smiled to myself at how independent she was becoming.

"I think I'm in love," I told Weston, sitting on his front step "With your daughter," I clarified.

"Oh, yeah...she is easy to fall in love with."

"Especially since I know she can't hurt me."

I drummed my fingers across my knee, not able to touch on why I was suddenly feeling so nervous.

"Weston?"

"Yes?"

"I don't want you to get upset with me, but does Olivia know things like her shapes and colors?"

"I don't know."

"What about the A-B-C song. You know, the one every parent teaches their kid?"

"I know the song," he said, rather serious.

"Does Olivia know it too?"

"I don't know. Ask Olivia. She is perfectly capable of answering," he grumbled.

"She didn't know."

"Why are you asking me all of this?"

"I was just looking up what she should know for her age and she doesn't seem to know a lot of it," I explained, remaining calm.

Oh no. I've upset him.

"So you think she is dumb?"

I cringed at the word *dumb*, turning around to see if Olivia was back yet and feeling relieved to find she wasn't.

"No, no, not at all. I just think that if she doesn't know, she should be taught because she will be going into kindergarten in just a couple of years."

"If watching her is too much for you then you can just tell me."

"Weston, please! I was simply just asking. I will teach her. I would love nothing more." Weston wouldn't even look at me. "Sorry, I won't bring it up again," I said, quietly.

"You just make me feel incompetent as a father. I'm doing the best I can," he seethed.

I reached across to place my hand on his, trying to gauge the level of hurt in his eyes.

"Weston, you are an amazing father. I will teach her! She is a very quick learner. Most kids are. She's brilliant," I exclaimed.

What an idiot I am. I had overstepped my boundaries and ruined our night.

I stayed quiet until Olivia returned and then I asked her if she flushed and washed her hands. She was all smiles and I was too when I felt her hands to see if they had just been washed. I think she was proud of herself, accomplishing the bathroom world all on her own and I was proud for her.

Neither Weston nor I spoke a word on our entire ride to the restaurant. I half expected him to just drive back home and was relieved when we pulled into the parking lot. Maybe I could somehow win back tonight.

I broke the silence when it was time to order. I so badly wanted Weston to speak to me, but the lack of conversation made it clear just how upset he was.

Our meal was served and we ate in silence. I wondered what I could say to snap Weston out of his bad mood. I guess I had hit a nerve the way Weston did to me the day before. I knew this was all a part of getting to know one another.

"Here's the money from our bet," I said after a while, placing a one-hundred-dollar bill in front of him. He didn't take the bait, continuing on in silence.

Come on! This is starting to get ridiculous.

Thank goodness for Olivia who gave a smile here and a giggle there while maneuvering through her macaroni and cheese. After we cleared our plates, Weston took out his wallet and placed his credit card on the table.

"Here's your check," the waitress said, waving the familiar black book which held our receipt.

"All set," Weston said, picking up his credit card from the table and handing it to the girl.

"Wow," the waitress said, scoffing up the one-hundred-dollar bill and holding it to her chest. "Thank you so much! You are beyond generous!"

When she left, both Weston and I burst out laughing.

"Who just grabs a hundred-dollar bill off the table and thinks it's theirs?" I asked, still laughing.

"Obviously that girl."

When we got into the truck, I finally broke the silence.

"I'm sorry for ruining our night."

"You didn't ruin anything. I know I'm not doing enough. I should be teaching her all this stuff. I'm just so busy with work. I don't know how to run a business and be a dad. I love her more than anything, though."

"I know. I hit a nerve and I didn't mean to."

He looked over at me and smiled.

"I want to help if you'll let me," I offered.

He nodded his head and took his eyes off the road to give me another glance. More and more I felt like I could squeeze my way into his life and feel right at home. When we pulled into the driveway, Olivia was asleep in the back.

"Do you want me to just keep her so you don't have to drive down here again tomorrow morning?"

He took a minute to think about it.

"Yeah," he said, hesitantly. "I just don't want to make it a habit."

"Or you'll hardly see her. I get it."

"It's just late at night. I already don't feel like much of a father. If she's sleeping here every night..."

"Weston, I get it. I promise."

"Okay, I'll help you get her into bed."

CHAPTER SIX

I took off my heels and tossed them onto the shoe rack filled with sneakers. I had no clue who they even belonged to. There were Nike basketball sneakers at least size twelve, so I was certain those weren't Sherri's. I looked forward to going through the house and donating anything that was no longer useful.

"Hey," Weston said as he eyed me looking at all the footwear.

"Hey. Who do these belong to?"

"Oh, probably us kids from over the years. Sherri held onto everything."

"So, what would I do if say I wanted to put all my shoes here?"

"Donate all of those. I told you, they're no use to us now. They might as well be useful to someone else."

"Okay. I think I'll start tomorrow if that's all right with you."

Weston let out a laugh. "Whatever you would like."

I smiled at him, sensing the feeling that he thought I was an exacerbating woman, but really I didn't want to step on anyone's toes.

"So, are you going to be okay all alone in this big house with just Olivia to keep you company?"

I nodded my head, looking down at the floor. Truthfully, I wanted him to stay. I didn't think someone was going to break in and hurt us. I didn't even think Travis would find me because I doubted he was even looking. I just wanted Weston to be here, but more than anything, I wanted him to want to be here and I knew his heart was telling him to go home. He had found himself in an odd circumstance knowing he had a house of his own.

"You feel safe here though, right?"

"Just go, catch a good night's rest."

"You aren't answering my question, Cora. Do you want me to stay? I can't do that couch anymore. I'm old."

I started laughing.

"Go, really!"

"Do you mean that or are you just saying that? I know females and you are an exhausting woman who cannot make eye contact when she lies."

I started pushing Weston backwards towards the door. I wore a smile, amused by his uncanny ability to sense I wanted him to stay. *He knows females? Why did every guy say that with pride?* Like we were some million-piece puzzle they finally solved.

"Yes I want you to stay because...ugh...I don't know why! I just feel better when you are here, but I don't like sleeping on the couch any more than you do, so just leave already!" I said jokingly as his back finally hit the door.

"I'll stay awhile."

"Please, I don't need to be coddled or tucked in at night. You wanted the truth so now you have it. Maybe I was just so used to being with someone for so long that it's hard to be alone."

"Maybe I've been alone for so long that it feels good to be in the company of someone," he said.

"How long have you been alone?"

"If we're going to have this conversation, I need a beer."

"Why does every guy say that? Athun just said that to me. What, guys can't talk? They have to have alcohol to open up?"

"Yeah, maybe."

He popped a beer and began drinking it.

"Want one?"

I shook my head no. I felt a physical attraction to Weston and knew the feelings would only heighten with alcohol. I didn't know if I wanted our relationship to go there though. I needed to work on myself for the time being.

"You watch TV?" he asked.

"Who doesn't?"

"I don't know. Let me have a beer or two while we watch television and then we can talk."

"I just don't understand how alcohol helps."

"Well, when you've never told a single soul how the love of your life died..."

"I didn't ask you that."

"That's where the conversation is headed, though. You want to know how many years I have been alone. It's been since Raina passed away."

"And you've never told a single soul, including your parents?"

"The nurse called them from the hospital."

"Other family members? Co-workers? Friends?"

"They just knew. I got the whole nine yards, the cards, the meals and all the 'sorry for your loss,' but I've never told anyone."

"Wow, that's remarkable."

"Remarkable?"

"No, sorry...wrong choice of words. I'm just surprised, that's all." I watched Weston sit there drinking his beer. "TV?"

Weston got up and went into Sherri's room, so I followed him.

"Why do we have to watch television in here?"

"It's the only television hooked up to cable. Sherri was a frugal woman; she didn't want to pay for two cable boxes."

I let out a laugh, running through the fond memories I had in my head of how frugal she truly was. She was a stay-at-home mom of two biological children and five step-children. I would think you would have to be frugal with that many kids. She never looked frugal, though. Maybe she got all her fancy clothing second hand.

I sat in bed next to Weston, feeling rather awkward. He kicked his shoes off and made himself right at home, turning on the television and stopping at the sports highlights. His love for sports still ran deep. After twenty minutes, he got up to retrieve another beer and sat back down.

"You're practically hanging off the bed. Are you afraid of me?"

"No," I lied. I was never usually this tense. On second thought, maybe I could loosen up like Weston if I drank a beer.

"I'm not going to try anything if that's what you are thinking."

"I know," I lied again and moved further onto the bed. I was starting to get cold and threw the covers over me. Just then he flicked off the sports channel and found some show. It looked familiar, but I couldn't remember the name of it.

"You ever watch this?" he asked.

"A long time ago. It's funny! I haven't seen it in a while."

After a few more minutes my eyes grew tired. I fought to stay awake as long as I could, but my body finally succumbed to sleep.

"Hey, you falling asleep on me?" Weston asked as he

turned the television off.

"Sorry," I mumbled, opening my eyes and finding him laying down on his side, looking at me.

I smiled at him and he smiled back. It felt like we were two teenagers, awkward and giddy.

"Tell me about her," I whispered. Weston rolled onto his back and looked up at the ceiling. "You don't have to if you don't want to."

"Raina was spectacular...a pure masterpiece. Her country was ruined by a hurricane and our company went there, to Antigua, to help them get back on their feet. When I first saw her, she was going through all her merchandise that had been ruined. There was hardly anything left, just the table still bolted to the ground and one shirt that had gotten caught on a bolt by the leg of the table. She spoke English, but I had a hard time understanding her accent. Truthfully, I think I fell in love with her that day...maybe even that very instant. She was beautiful, unlike any woman I had ever seen, which is funny because she was so sad. She was crying.

Anyway, I checked on her every day while we were there, which was for almost a month. On the last day, I dug up the courage and asked her if she wanted to come to America with me. She did. We got married shortly after. She got her green card and I got her a job with my sisters in the office. At first, she didn't think she could be of any help, but I asked my sisters to be patient with her. She caught on rather quickly and she became a part of our family in no time.

We got pregnant with Olivia right away. The pregnancy was rough from the beginning. Raina was sick throwing up every day. I even had to bring her to the hospital for an IV because she was so dehydrated. When it came time to give birth, Raina wanted it to be all natural. She did beautifully. I brought her to the hospital at six centimeters dilated. The nurse taught me how to do this pressure point technique on her lower back, so I did with every contraction."

I turned towards him, laying on my side. I was hanging on his every word.

"After Olivia was born, they took her to be examined. I'll never forget hearing her first cry. I started crying because I was so happy. Raina's placenta hadn't detached, so they gave her medicine right away to help. Twenty minutes later and it still wasn't working. Raina was having contractions again from the medicine. The doctor was pushing down on her lower stomach, trying to manually detach the placenta, but that wasn't working either. There was a lot of blood, but after a while it was like it just started pouring out of her. I was up by Raina's head at that point, so I couldn't see much. Raina stayed calm, she wasn't panicking or anything, but she was in so much pain.

As time went on, I knew something was seriously wrong. The doctor began calling out orders and his tone had completely changed. The nurse went to get more nurses and they started running around. Raina's lips started to turn this ashy grey color. I didn't know what to think...I mean, we were in a goddamn hospital. They save people every day, not let them die!

After some time Raina's face went completely white, like a ghost. Two nurses ripped me off her. I put up a good fight. I struggled to stay right there by her side. The doctor stepped in and they practically threw me into the hallway and shut the door, locking it. I kicked the shit out of the door and eventually security took me away. I knew that was it. She was gone. I never got to hold her while she died. She died scared and alone. I hate that hospital. I hate that doctor and I hate all those nurses."

I started crying, overcome with sadness. It was like Weston's pain was radiating off his body and right into my heart.

"I've read this happening a thousand times to mothers giving birth, but I swear to God it could have been prevented. There was no reason for her to die. They have so much technology now...so many different medicines. Now I just feel like I brought Raina here to die. If she never met me, she would still be alive in Antigua and selling t-shirts to tourists on the street."

"Don't say that! You don't know that Weston."

"And how can my worst day also be my favorite? Raina gave me Olivia, the reason I still get up out of bed every morning. Olivia saved me and she made me keep going."

I moved closer to Weston's side while shaking my head. When he turned his head, we were forehead to forehead. We both closed our eyes in the moment and took a deep breath. I quickly moved to his chest, completely terrified by our intimacy, but feeling the need to console him.

"I'm so sorry, Weston." I wrapped my arm up over his chest. He didn't hold me back.

"You know what the worst part was?"

"What?"

"I'm a man, which means I'm not allowed to cry. I'm supposed to be strong. Nobody helped me, Cora. My parents or siblings...nobody stopped by the house to check on me or help with Olivia. I was just left on my own."

I didn't know what to say to him.

"Even you didn't ask me about her. It's like nobody cares..."

I propped myself up on one elbow and looked at him.

"Now that's not true! I didn't ask because it's none of my business. That doesn't mean I wasn't wondering where she was or what happened to her. I have a heart, Weston."

"I know. I just feel like nobody even remembers her. Her birthday comes and goes and the day she died comes and goes and nobody ever says a word. They say happy birthday to Olivia, but doesn't anyone remember Raina?"

"Of course they do. Some people just don't know how to deal with death. Maybe they don't know how to talk about Raina when they're around you."

"I'm not fragile; I feel things."

"Maybe they're fragile...maybe they are still in pain, too."

"Maybe."

"Are you angry with everyone who you thought would be there more and wasn't?" I asked.

"Yes."

"Well maybe you should give people the benefit of the doubt. If you asked your parents or your siblings to be there, would they have been?"

"Yeah, in a heartbeat. We are always there for each other, but death...I shouldn't have to ask."

"Maybe that's the way you feel, but that might not be how they feel, right?"

"I guess, when you put it that way."

"If you want something, you should always ask."

"Isn't that the pot calling the kettle black? Just an hour or so ago you were pushing me out the door when you really wanted me to stay."

"I just feel like I shouldn't feel the way I do. I want you to stay, but you aren't my boyfriend, so it's weird if you do."

"I feel the same way, like I should go when I really want to stay."

I laid there on his chest smiling.

"Cora?"

"Yeah?"

"What do you want from me?"

"What do you mean?"

"You know what I mean."

"I don't want anything from you, Weston. I enjoy your company and whatever you're doing right now is perfect."

I didn't know if what I was saying was a lie or the truth. He didn't say a word after that. I was mesmerized by the rise and fall of his chest and listening to the rhythm of his heartbeat. In that moment, I felt like my life was imperfectly perfect. Weston had opened up to me, which meant I meant something to him. Somehow tonight, I felt like we grew closer.

What did I want from him? I wasn't ready for a relationship, but maybe someday I could be. I didn't want to rush things like I had with Travis. It was all too easy to ruin the perfect time I was having. I closed my eyes and fell asleep.

****

I was turned away from where Weston laid the night before, snuggling a pile of blankets. I wondered momentarily if Weston pushed me off him or if I had gone willingly. Weston was no longer in bed. I checked the time and it was just past six in the morning. I tiptoed out of bed and checked the driveway, Weston's truck was gone. I started a pot of coffee and returned to bed, surfing the internet on my phone until Oliva woke up. A message popped up on my phone from Weston.

"Do something for me?"

I sat up, intrigued to find what Weston wanted. I typed out "Anything...", then deleted that and typed out "What's up?" *Send*!

"Go strawberry picking with Olivia and I, this afternoon?"

"I'd love to." It was all I could do to contain my excitement. I got out of bed, far too thrilled to spend another minute lying around.

Olivia and I spent the morning cleaning. She was such a

great little helper! I poured my affection onto her, giving her hugs and kisses throughout the day. She greedily ate up my attention for her, sitting in my lap and asking me to sleep with her again when it came time for her nap. When I met her just a week ago, I would have told you she is serious and shy, but now she had opened up to me. I tease her and she giggles. I tickle her until she screams with uncontrollable laughter.

"Hey, you girls ready?" I heard a voice whisper. I opened my eyes and found Weston in the doorway, that smile instantly bringing life to every inch of my body.

"We are," I said, watching Olivia open her eyes and smile at Weston when she realized Daddy was home. "We just have to get our shoes on."

I hadn't been strawberry picking since I was a kid. I couldn't wait to get into the kitchen and bake every possible strawberry dessert I could think of. I wanted the house to smell like a strawberry rhubarb pie. There was something so incredibly wholesome about picking your own fruit and turning it into all sorts of masterpieces for all to enjoy. I had almost forgotten about all the little aspects of life that used to fulfill me as a child. Whether Weston knew it or not, he was teaching me a great deal about the little things that left a huge impact in my life.

"You want your own container?" Weston asked.

"Oh yeah, I want a ton of strawberries! I'll pay for myself, though."

He shook his head, asking the cashier for a few more berry baskets.

We took a hayride out to the field. I was so excited, letting the breeze blow my unruly hair across my face as I inhaled the fresh air. I caught Weston and the others looking at me, probably wondering what I was so happy about.

When we found our spot, I took Olivia's hand and we

ventured to the biggest strawberries I could find. I turned back and looked for Weston.

"Sorry, I'm not trying to take over. You probably want to do this with her."

"Don't be sorry. I wouldn't have invited you if I didn't want you here with us."

So he wants me here...

"I feel like everyone is looking at us. What do you think they're thinking, two white parents with an adopted kid?" I asked, starting to fill a container.

"You haven't stopped smiling since we got in the truck. Seriously, they're all wondering how your cheeks don't hurt from smiling so much."

"Stop!"

"What are you so giddy about, anyway?"

"I needed this today, more than you know."

"Me too," he said, plucking a giant strawberry and handing it to Olivia. The gesture had my heart fluttering. I didn't just fall for Olivia, I was falling for Weston, too and the meaning behind the two of them together. I took out my phone and snapped a few pictures, sending them to Weston.

"Would you like me to take a picture of all of you?" I heard a man ask from behind me.

"Ah...sure..." I gave the man my phone and then leaned in with Weston and Olivia.

"Beautiful family. Enjoy the rest of your day," he said.

"Thanks." I looked at the picture. I smiled, then instantly felt guilty Raina wasn't here to enjoy her family and even guiltier knowing I very much wanted to be a part of it.

CHAPTER SEVEN

Weeks turned into a month and now Olivia was starting to feel like a part of me. Weston would come home every day and usually find us sleeping. I loved my and Olivia's afternoon nap. After I'd wake, I'd start dinner and we would eat like a family. I tested all my favorite meals out on them first, so they thought I was this amazing cook. After those meals got boring, I tried a new recipe every night, repeating those Olivia and Weston raved about.

Each night, Weston and I would roll into bed next to one another and watch television or talk. Sometimes we were so tired we would just go to bed. There was never any physical contact. Well, maybe there was in our sleep, but none on purpose at least. Weston would gravitate towards me in the night and hold me closely, so I would let him. In the morning, he would be gone and we never spoke about it.

I never tried anything because I knew Weston's heart was still with Raina and probably always would be. My heart would still be with Travis, if his heart wasn't in love with drugs. We had found ourselves in the oddest of most odd relationships, but it was working rather well at the moment.

Then again, at this very moment Travis was calling me like he had every day this past week. He left a voicemail every time, but I refused to listen to them. I knew exactly what he wanted. It was nearing the first of the month which meant the mortgage was due.

"Your phone has been ringing an awful lot lately," Weston said one day.

"Travis. He's just looking for me to pay the bills."

"Well, are you?"

"Of course."

"Can I ask why?"

"I told you the first day I came here that I'd never want to be the reason he was homeless. And truthfully, I guess it makes me feel less guilty walking out on him."

"I get that you don't want to talk to him, but if you know what he wants then why don't you just tell him you've got it covered?"

"I don't know. I'm not ready to face that part of my life just yet."

"Okay, but it wouldn't hurt to let the guy know."

"Hey! Whose side are you on here?"

"Definitely yours, but maybe then he'd stop calling," he said, smirking.

Weston was probably right. After giving it some thought, I typed out a message to Travis. I saved it in my phone for two more days before sending it.

"Travis, I don't know what to say to you right now, which is why I haven't been answering your phone calls. Every time I see your name flash across the screen on my phone, all I think about is our failed marriage. I need some space right now to process everything. I will continue to pay the mortgage and utility bills. I've already set them up on automatic payment. I ask that you respect my wishes and just give me time."

When I finally had the courage to send it, I closed my eyes and said a silent prayer to God, begging for Travis to listen to me. I didn't even want to think about a divorce or anything else to do with him at this moment in my life.

A few months later I started feeling like I was ready to get back on the market. Every day throughout the summer I would take Olivia to the bike trail. It was her favorite place to be. I would bring flashcards and we would have a picnic. I taught her everything under the sun, from one through twenty to the entire alphabet. We had almost completed her colors. She now knew things like elbow, throat and knee cap. She was a clever little girl and I rewarded her with a trip to the ice cream shop every week.

It was there, on the bike trail, I would run into Athun. It was like a daily routine, bike path, picnic, teaching Olivia and a small chat with Athun while Olivia admired his dog. I was starting to realize that I really had nothing to lose finding my way back into Athun's heart. If he could love me before, certainly he could love me again because it was clear things were never going to go anywhere with Weston. After all this time, I wasn't any closer to moving out of his friend zone.

Just then, Weston appeared.

"Hey, I saw your truck parked in the lot. I figured I'd walk the path until I found you and Olivia and...here you are."

Olivia squealed and jumped into her father's arms. "Daddy, Moose!" she shrieked, pointing to Athun's dog.

"That's his name," I teased, pointing to the dog and smiling. "And this is Athun." They exchanged greetings.

"I have some time in between clients today, so I was going to see if you girls wanted to do lunch."

"We just ate actually."

Athun excused himself, saying something to the effect of

finishing his walk with Moose. I was too busy eyeing Weston, trying to figure out why he looked so perplexed staring at Athun.

"Tonight?" Athun hollered.

"Tonight," I called back. Weston kept his eyes on Athun until he was out of sight, then he turned to me.

"Your gyno friend?"

"Yeah. He's a great guy!"

"So what, you two meet here every day or something?"

"Kind of. He walks Moose here and I bring Olivia to have a picnic. This is her favorite place."

"What about a playground or something more geared towards a three-year-old?" His demeanor had shifted to a more serious one now.

"I never even thought to take her to a playground. I can do that! You don't like the bike path?"

"I don't like that she's around some guy I don't know," he said, crossing his arms in defense.

"I see Athun in passing, five minutes tops and besides, he's harmless. I would never have Olivia near anyone I thought would hurt her." I stared at him, but his eyes never met my gaze.

"What is this about? Me or Olivia?" I asked, placing my hands on my hips.

"I don't know."

What?

"Athun doesn't like me like that!"

"Oh please, I saw the way he looks at you."

"So, this *is* about me then?"

"I don't want to talk about it right now."

"Let me guess, you need a beer? I have one in my back pocket," I joked, sarcastically. Right then Olivia decided to butt in, singing the alphabet.

"That was beautiful, Olivia. Did Cora teach you that song?"

Weston asked.

She nodded her head and then counted to twenty, forgetting to say fifteen. Weston was beyond impressed.

"Wow, you smart little girl! What else has Cora taught you?"

"That the sky is blue," she said, pointed to the sky. "The grass is green." She crouched down low and ran her hand over the blades of grass. "This right here is black," she said, tapping her foot on the asphalt. I was smiling from ear to ear, so proud of the progress Olivia had made in such a short time.

"C'mon pretty girl," he said, scooping Olivia up into his arms and planting a kiss on her cheek.

"Cora said you already ate so I'll treat you both to some ice cream."

We climbed into Weston's truck and ventured to our treat. Weston explained his last appointment was supposed to be half a days' worth of work and they had cancelled, which is why he had come looking for us. I just sat there wondering why in the world Athun bothered him.

"Can we talk about Athun?"

"Just forget about it."

"No. I go to the bike path because Olivia loves to see the dogs. That's where I taught her everything she just showed you. I love our time there, but if you don't want us to go there anymore, then we won't."

"Forget about it," he repeated.

"You are SO frustrating sometimes," I said, through clenched teeth.

Weston didn't say a word. I'm sure he didn't want to have this conversation in front of Olivia, but I was rather bothered by his remarks from earlier. When we turned into the ice cream place, I shifted my body towards him.

"What do you want from me?"

"To take care of Olivia while I'm at work."

"That's all?"

"That's all." I felt like Weston had wound up and gave me a swift kick to my ribs. I breathed in deep and exhaled. I suddenly wished that his last appointment had never gotten cancelled. The daily routine Olivia and I had was perfect. I didn't want to jump to different playgrounds around town and chat with moms. I didn't want to let Olivia free to go play with the other kids while I sit on some bench watching. I wanted to be the one to entertain her and to bond with her.

Ugh! I foolishly mistook his words for jealousy, which made me think he wanted more. For those very few minutes, I shined brighter and now I had a hard time hiding my disappointment. In fact, I was mad as hell!

The truth was, I felt conflicted and I'd be lying if I said I didn't have feelings for both Weston and Athun. Inside my heart, I still had this slight inclination that Weston was jealous of Athun. He showed up playing Mr. Macho man and it was rather unattractive. Of course, Weston had to be feeling something towards me other than nothing. We played house together and he seemed to enjoy that just as much as I did.

I decided to play the silent game because I had nothing to say to him. When he dropped me back off at my truck at the bike trail, I told him I wouldn't be home until late.

Screw him!

I played the retail therapy game for a few hours before heading over to Athun's house. I found Athun in the kitchen preparing baked spaghetti.

"Wow, you are quite the chef! I could get used to this." And just like that, all my frustration from earlier was gone.

As the night went on, I was completely distracted, only

half listening to Athun's stories from high school. I was busy wondering what Olivia had eaten for dinner, if anything. It was so hard to draw that line between playing the babysitter role and "mommy", because I felt more like her mother. I called it an early night with Athun and headed home.

As I made my way inside, I saw the glow of the television from our bedroom. I went inside, finding Weston sitting up in bed. He held his hand out for me and I went to him, noticing several beer cans on the nightstand.

"Sit," he whispered and I obliged. "I don't want to fight."

He ran his hand over the top of my head and cradled my face. His hand was warm. We were so close...I could feel his breath on my face. I leaned in to kiss him and he kissed me back.

"I'm sorry. I just can't," he said, backing away.

"Can't or won't?"

"Both."

I stood up, feeling wounded. I was a fool for leaving Athun. I should've stayed at his house and had my self-esteem soaring instead of having Weston cut it down...again.

I left the bedroom and went to the couch. I grabbed the blanket off the back and threw the pillow to the end, laying down and letting the hurt stream down my face. I just wanted to know where life was going to take me. I didn't know how long I could watch Olivia for or how long I could sleep next to her father, wanting more, but never getting it. If I stayed, I'd be setting myself up for an emotional rollercoaster. Hell, I already was.

****

I set up plans with Athun as soon as the afternoon approached. I didn't want to be home with Weston tonight. I went about my day, preparing to leave right when Weston came home. I kept things between us brief and left before he could start in about the night before, if he was even planning on acknowledging it.

I stopped on my way to Athun's and bought a bikini. It was quite revealing, particularly on my rear end, but I didn't care. I craved something different from the norm. Besides, in my eyes I still had a gorgeous body and it was time I showed it off. Athun would be the perfect person since I knew he wouldn't have eyes for my skin and bones.

Athun offered me a beer as soon as I arrived and I took it greedily, along with a second and third. I was feeling a little buzzed now, which is what I needed if I wanted to push Weston and Olivia to the back of my mind and focus on Athun tonight.

We ate dinner and then it was time to reveal my new swimsuit, trying desperately to be proud of my body. I was so nervous I tripped on my way into the hot tub and landed on Athun's lap.

"Tipsy?"

"No, I planned that," I said, giggling. I wiped the water from Athun's face. Feeling rather bold from the alcohol, I leaned in and introduced my lips to his. There was no rejection. A fury within both of us erupted. Athun wanted me just as much as I wanted him. I reached my hand up his leg, signaling I wanted more.

"We can't do that here!" Athun said, breaking our kiss.

"Why? You have no neighbors!"

"You shouldn't have sex in a hot tub because you could..."

"Is this about my lady business?"

"Yes, you could get a..."

"No! I don't want to hear it! You can't teach me about something you don't even have."

He backed his hands up in defense.

"Okay, just trying to help. We can move this to my bedroom..."

"Yes! The bedroom. Is it safe there?" I asked, sarcastically.

"No more chatter. You're always safe with me. Don't think about this...just do it. We're both adults. You were my best friend and I've wanted this for years."

I stripped my bathing suit off when we reached Athun's room. Goosebumps rippled my arms. I was suddenly freezing.

"Can we shower? I'm so cold."

Athun started smirking. He turned on a light and entered a room off his bedroom. I followed him, giggling nervously. It was the bathroom. He started the shower and stepped in with his swimming trunks still on.

"Are you coming?" he asked.

"Not with your bathing suit still on! It's not fair. I'm completely naked right now!"

"Very funny. C'mon, I just want to look at you," he said, reaching out for me and pulling me in. I tried convincing myself to have confidence as I stood there before him, completely exposed.

"No, you're judging me and I hate it."

"I am not."

"Am I normal? Do I look like all the others?" I joked.

"Cora, you are much more beautiful than any patient I have ever had in my exam room."

"You have to say that or I won't sleep with you." Athun let out a laugh.

"I have a weird question and I don't want to upset you," he said.

"Oh no, what?"

"Why are your nipples so incredibly dark? Are they always like that?"

My jaw literally dropped to the floor. *Was he being*

serious? I looked down at my nipples. *What the hell*...they were a dark chocolate brown. I had never noticed it before.

"What could that mean?" I asked.

I was trying to measure his facial expression. His face wore wrinkles from his forehead down to his nose.

"Are you pregnant?"

Athun's words knocked the wind out of me. It was a complete libido shut down. I swallowed hard before I answered. Travis was the only other soul who knew the answer.

"I was..."

"How long ago?"

"Almost eight years."

"Oh. No, that wouldn't be it. What I meant was, could you be pregnant right now?"

I shook my head, trying to remember the last time I had slept with anyone. It was Travis, five months ago...days before I left. We didn't use protection. I felt like I was going to be sick. I swung open the shower door and stepped out, grabbing the first towel I had to hide my body from Athun. I started panicking now. I knew I had to be pregnant. I was tired all the time. Although I wasn't ever nauseous...not that I could remember anyway. The tired is what led me to believe I *was* pregnant. I had been zombie tired for quite some time, which is why my daily nap with Olivia was perfect.

"I'm sorry I said anything. It's just, your skin is so fair," Athun explained, interrupting my thoughts.

"I need to go get a pregnancy test...right...now!" I choked. I felt like I could barely breathe.

"I'll take you."

Athun drove me to the local convenience store where I bought three different tests. Athun laughed when I returned to his vehicle and saw what I had done.

"I told you which one would be efficient."

"I know. I'm just freaking out! I need to know without a doubt if I'm pregnant or not."

When we got back to Athun's house, I went to his bathroom right away and took all three tests. All three were positive. I…was…pregnant. Athun found me on the floor of the bathroom crying.

"Tonight is the worst night. We were just going to have sex and now here I am, knocked up. I know what you are thinking about me right now."

"I'm not passing any judgement, believe me."

"No, you're thinking, 'Thank God it's not mine.'"

"Not at all, Cora. That thought never even entered my mind. Who's the father? Olivia's dad?"

"Gosh no! He wouldn't touch me with a ten-foot pole. It's Travis's baby. He went on this 'I'm sober' rant and I started thinking he really changed. When he relapsed again, I left that night."

"So what are you going to do?"

"I can't have another abortion."

Oops.

"I guess the cat is out of the bag on that one, so now you know all my deepest darkest secrets. I bet you're really judging me now."

"I am not. I'm sure you had the perfect reason."

"I did. I didn't want the baby's father to be addicted to heroin, which is what would have happened if I didn't have an abortion."

Athun leaned in and kissed me on the head.

"Don't feel like you have to explain yourself to me," he said.

"I'm not so perfect now, am I?"

Athun took my face in his hands. “You are perfect in my eyes.” He kissed me on the lips, a soft, slow, sincere kiss.

“Thank you for that.”

“You’re welcome,” he said smiling. “So, are you going to tell anyone?”

“No. Not yet anyway. I think the best thing to do is give it up for adoption. Travis doesn’t know I’m pregnant this time and I’d be setting myself up for failure raising a child with no father. Every child needs a mother and father. Why are you looking at me like that?”

“No reason, I’m just listening. I’m behind you whatever decision you make.”

“Thanks.”

“Can I do my doctor speech now?”

“Out with it Doctor Lom,” I said, waving my hand in the air.

“You need to start on a prenatal vitamin right away. It may constipate you, so a daily stool softener is fine. Also, if it upsets your stomach during the day, then it’s perfectly okay to take it at night. I can prescribe one for you or you can easily buy one over the counter.”

“Okay. Thank you, Doctor Lom. Is there anything else?”

“Yes, I will see you in my office tomorrow. We will need to see how far along you are.”

“No way! Didn’t you say that girl Erin we graduated with is one of your secretaries? She is such a gossip queen! There’s absolutely no way I’m coming to your office.”

“You want me to steal my equipment and bring it home with me?”

“No, of course not! I’ll go somewhere else.”

“C’mon! I’m the best gynecologist in the Midwest. Seeing someone else would be a complete insult.”

“Then prepare to be insulted.”

"You are quite the stubborn woman."

"I'm hormonal."

****

When I arrived home, I was surprised to find Weston's truck in the driveway. I wondered how odd it must be for him to own two houses now, bouncing from one to the other. I wondered what he had told his neighbor about no longer needing her babysitting services for Olivia. His neighbors must be curious as to why they no longer see him.

I opened the drawer to retrieve my pajamas and found it filled with Weston's clothes. *When had he done this?* Certainly not tonight. Maybe after our fight. I opened the next one down and found some more. *Was he slowly moving from his house into this one?* Now more than ever I was confused.

I slid into bed next to a sleeping Weston, unable to fathom how Athun knew I was pregnant with one glance at my body and I had no idea. Yes, my breasts were sore, but I just contributed that to my period coming. I had been so busy with uprooting my world halfway across the country that I hadn't paid much attention to my period being late. I remember it dawning on me once or twice, but I blamed it on stress.

My second pregnancy and I still wasn't in a position to raise a child.

I felt like such a loser. I just started getting my life together and now this was another setback. I just wanted a normal life. My last thought before I succumbed to sleep was hooking up the camper and leaving Iowa for good.

CHAPTER EIGHT

I called an obstetrician gynecology office an hour away. Was I being paranoid here? I didn't want to run into anyone I knew and especially not anyone who knew my parents. I was too worried about gossip girl Erin working in Athun's office. There was just no way I could go there! The earliest appointment they had was a week away. I booked it, although I wasn't sure I could wait that long. I would certainly chew off all my fingernails by then!

Athun texted me mid-morning asking me to meet him on his lunch break at his house. I pictured myself walking through his door and finding a boat load of maternity necessities. He seemed to be quite passionate when it came to being a doctor. I felt bad judging him, based solely on the fact that he's a man. There were plenty of females working in this field that I had met along the way that weren't nearly as avid as Athun.

I packed a lunch for me and Olivia and off we went to Athun's. Olivia squealed for Moose as soon as she saw him.

"What is so important? Your text sounded urgent," I said, as soon as Athun answered the door.

"I just wanted to make sure you weren't going to go see another doctor today."

"They can't take me for another week."

"You made an appointment?"

"Yes."

"With whom?"

"I don't know, someone an hour away. That's all I really care about!"

"You don't even know the name of the doctor you are entrusting your health and wellness to?"

"Well when you put it that way, you make me feel irresponsible."

"You are a wicked woman! Come," he said, ushering us through the door.

I followed him to his living room, finding an exam table set up with what looked like an ultrasound probe.

"No…you…didn't."

"I did!" he said, looking quite pleased with himself. "It just didn't feel right that you would go to someone else when I am perfectly capable. I see you almost every day, Cora!"

I was somewhat amused and a little taken aback by Athun's sweet gesture.

"Thank you," I said, reaching my arms up around his neck and squeezing him hard.

"Olivia, do you want to see a baby?"

"Athun!" I scolded him.

"What? Kids love this stuff. I encourage mothers to bring their children to their ultrasound appointments all the time. Now, are you ready to see how far along you are?"

My head began racing with thoughts as I watched Athun scoop up Olivia and place her on his lap. Oh no! What if she tells Weston?

"Lay down on the table," Athun instructed.

"Are you sure this thing is going to hold me?"

"It's one of those traveling masseuse tables, it's fine."

"Where did you get it?"

"Don't worry about that!"

"How did you get this stuff here anyway?"

He gave me a look like I was an idiot.

"I know how you got it...from your office, but how did you get it without anyone saying anything?"

"Don't you worry about that either. Now, lay your head down and pull down your pants. You might have to pull your underwear down a little too. I'm going to squirt some gel on you, but I didn't have time to warm it so I apologize."

"I think cold gel is the least of my problems." We both laughed.

"Okay Olivia, this here is an iPad that'll help us see the baby. We'll plug this probe into the iPad and we're good to go! Take the little wand here," Athun told her, handing her the probe. "Now swish it around until we find the little peanut. Oop, here we go, I found a hand. Do you girls see it?"

He pointed to an object on the screen. I had no problem making out the baby's hand with tiny little fingers.

"Hand," Olivia gushed.

"There you are baby...relaxing in momma's belly." Athun and Olivia seemed to be enjoying themselves, but just the word momma made me anxious. The last thing I planned on being right now was a mother.

"So, it looks like you are measuring at twenty-five weeks. Does that sound right?"

"Honestly, I haven't a clue."

"That's five months and two weeks. Your due date is January 12th."

"Ugh, I'll probably have to drive to the hospital during a snowstorm!"

"So…you are going to deliver?" Athun asked as he placed Olivia back on her feet and helped me sit up.

"I told you, I'll never do what I did ever again. It still haunts me."

"The past is in the past. Shut that door, Cora."

"I know. Maybe someday I'll be able to."

"I have to get back to work. I have been extra suspicious today!"

"You mean, you're normally a suspicious doctor?" Athun started laughing.

"I don't know what my staff thinks of me, but I was definitely a little suspicious today. Look, will you let me take care of you throughout your progression? I'll bring all this back to the office, but I'll bring it back in a couple months when I need to check you again."

"Don't I have to have some blood tests?"

"There's a test that checks for things like down syndrome, trisomy 21 and spina bifida, but sadly that's first trimester screening. There's a blood glucose test I will need to do, which I do between twenty-four to twenty-eight weeks so we'll set that up within the next week or two."

"I don't know. Will you be the one personally drawing my blood?"

"Yes. You can come to my office after hours."

"I-I don't want to get you in any trouble, Athun."

"Nonsense, it's my practice. I do as I see fit."

"And you want to do all this, even though I am giving the baby up for adoption?"

"I'm not focusing on where the baby ends up. I am focusing on you and making sure the baby is healthy."

"Okay."

"Yes?" he asked.

"Yes."

"So, you will cancel that appointment, you know, with that other doctor you found online?"

"Yes, Doctor. Right away, Doctor."

He looked at me with a devilish grin. He was exhausting and charming at the same time. I loved the looks he gave me.

"I have to go," he said, zipping up his bag with the ultrasound machine in it and kissing me on the head. "Stay. Just lock up when you're finished."

"Okay."

I watched him walk out the front door.

"Thank you, Athun," I called after him. He was cleverly finding his way into my heart. I stood up, pulling up my pants and looking at my stomach. I hardly looked pregnant. I remember with the first pregnancy, the midwife telling me it would be quite some time before I would start showing because of how tall I was. I was five foot seven inches. The uterus grows up until it reaches your belly button, before you start growing out. I can remember that conversation like it was yesterday. She told me I had twenty-one weeks before I'd start showing. I never did start showing because I had my abortion before then. This time, I would certainly be able to watch my belly swell.

We strolled through Athun's house until we found Moose. Olivia immediately laid down on the ground and curled up into him.

"You really like dogs, don't you?"

"This one."

"I can see that."

"You ready for lunch, my sweet girl?"

"Yes."

"Let's go to a playground. We'll eat lunch, play a little bit and then we'll go take a nap." I was already starting to feel tired.

"Give Moose a kiss and we'll see him tomorrow."

Olivia said her goodbyes and off we went. The playground was empty, not another soul around. Olivia was slow maneuvering across the bridge and scared to go down the slide. She was even overly cautious on the swings. It's like Olivia had been hiding under a rock her whole life because everywhere I took her was a new experience for her. I found myself pumping my legs as hard as I could with Olivia on my lap. She giggled in my ear, screaming when she looked down and saw how high up we were.

"Don't look down!" I told her. "Cora won't let you get hurt."

After the swings, I showed Olivia how to use the monkey bars. Then, I lifted her up on my shoulders so she could try. We went down every slide on the playground multiple times. Olivia took all my stress away. She was so much fun and so very innocent. Gosh, was she innocent. She pulled on my heartstrings daily, without even trying.

She was fast asleep in the back seat when we arrived home. I whispered in her ear as we headed up the stairs.

"Olivia?" She opened her eyes. "You make me so happy."

She grabbed my face and smiled. It was in that moment my love for her was confirmed. I placed her down in her bed and tiptoed out. I had a new plan inside my head. While Olivia napped every day, I would make dinner for her and Weston. When Weston arrived home, I would leave to see Athun. I wasn't mad at Weston, I just wanted more. If it wasn't for this little chicklet growing inside my body, I could've seen myself being with him. It didn't matter anymore though, because he *couldn't*.

I wasn't sure if I could see myself with Athun. Athun was a family man. He needed a wife who wanted lots of children. He had his act together and I was far from playing the leading role.

I was two loads of laundry in, the smell of dinner roaming throughout the house when Weston walked through the door.

"It smells delicious in here. What are you cooking?"

"Just some meatballs." He turned on the oven light and peered in.

"There's not a whole lot. I could eat all of those," he said, looking confused.

"I have a lot of errands I have to run. You and Olivia eat without me."

"What about when you come back home?"

"I'll eat dinner at Athun's house."

"Oh. Is that where you've been going now?"

"Yeah. I like spending time with him."

"And not with us?"

"Things have just been weird between us. You and I, we weren't going to cross that line and then we did. Which was fine. I could have done without the rejection, though."

"Cora, I wasn't rejecting you."

"You literally pushed me off you like I was repulsive. Do you know how that makes me feel?"

"I just..."

"Honestly, I don't really care to hear what you have to say. It's not going to change anything. I don't mind cooking dinner for you and Olivia every night. Besides, she should have her alone time with her daddy. I love her, Weston. She's changed my life in a way I never thought possible. Today, I spent my time going down the slides at the playground and swinging as high as I could with her on my lap laughing. I never thought this is where I would be in life. She makes me so happy."

Tears started forming in my eyes.

Hormones!

"I always think how crazy it is that one tiny human being

could fill up such a big part of my heart," Weston said, smiling.

"You're doing such a great job," I told him.

"Me? Please, I owe it all to you. I've seen such a change in her since you've been around. Her speech is much better and she's so friendly when we go out now. Before you she was petrified! Her favorite place was behind my leg. She's outgoing now and that has nothing to do with me, Cora."

"It's getting colder lately, but I think I'll keep bringing her to the playground because I noticed she had a lot of fears today. I mean, when she goes to school, there's going to be recess. I don't want her to be the kid that sits on the side because she's afraid of a slide. I want her to make friends."

"Thank you," he said.

"For what?"

"For being you. I wish you would stay and eat with us."

"I can't. I just need an emotional break right now."

"Because of me?"

"I guess...yeah...maybe. I better go now," I said, and off I went before I said something I would later regret. It was right then I wanted to turn and give him every reason to give us a chance, but the truth was, I couldn't even think of one.

CHAPTER NINE

I was wearing a big smile on my face when I found Athun in the kitchen preparing dinner.

"What are you so happy about?" he asked.

"You. You are amazing!"

"Yeah, how so?"

"You've always treated me like a princess. I love that. And now, you're all grown up and cooking dinner every night."

"Actually, I never really enjoyed cooking dinner. It's nice to have someone I can cook for."

"You can cook for me anytime you want."

"Yeah, this can be our nightly ritual. I love your company."

"Well, I will give you my company until some young beautiful woman stumbles upon you and steals you away from me."

Athun stopped what he was doing and looked at me.

"I was hoping that young beautiful woman would be you."

Huh?

"Athun, I am SIX months pregnant! I am about to turn into a cow and then have a bowling ball of a baby pass through my vagina. I am no good."

"I find pregnancy to be a beautiful thing. Every time I deliver a baby, I'm really delivering a miracle."

"Achy back, swollen ankles and the waddle. Oh, the waddle."

"I love it all," he gushed.

"Really?"

"Yes. I think you are remarkable and you make a beautiful pregnant woman. You need to stop looking at it like it is a chore and start realizing that pregnancy is a blessing. Some women try for years to get pregnant. They spend thousands of dollars trying out every different medicine and procedure we have available. Still they fail. You are blessed," he said, leaning in and kissing me softly on my lips. The feeling was odd and unfamiliar. I didn't understand why Athun wanted to wait for me to be baby free. Then, on top of that, I had several months to get my body back into shape. Some books I have read says it takes a whole year for your body to return to normal.

From that day forward, Athun and I were a thing. We held hands and kissed. He didn't understand why I would never let us go farther than kissing, but I was starting to show and was very insecure about my body. My breasts had increased at least one cup size and I looked bloated, like I ate a big lunch. Thankfully, I was still able to hide my pregnancy from Weston by wearing sweatshirts.

When the Iowa weather turned bitterly cold, Olivia and I were forced to stay inside. I would meet Athun for lunch at his house every day and Olivia was beyond excited to visit Moose. She taught him paw and how to sit. I loved watching how proud she was of herself. Athun would watch what I ate, always pushing fruits and vegetables on me. The look on his face when I unwrapped my deli sub today was a look I will never forget.

"Cold deli meat. Cora, this isn't cooked! Didn't you read

any of the paperwork I gave you?"

"Yes, Doctor. I never saw anything about deli sandwiches."

"It's right next to hot dogs. You can't have them!"

"Hot dogs? You've got to be kidding me."

"No, they can actually change the figure of the baby's face."

"No way! What else can't I eat?"

"Sushi."

"Stop right there! Sushi is my favorite and you've already taken away alcohol. You're not much fun, you know."

"I am a lot of fun. Please, you're in your last trimester now."

"Three long months of no sushi, alcohol, deli meat, hot dogs and oh...limiting my caffeine."

I inched closer to him, kissing his forehead, then his cheeks and his lips.

"No, Cora, you can't eat this," he said, tossing my sub into the trash.

"I could've just cooked it, Athun!"

"Sorry. I already threw it away," he said, shrugging his shoulders.

"Well, I guess I'm leaving now so I can go feed my baby something else."

"You're leaving? I'll make you something."

"Goodbye, Athun." I snatched Olivia up in a hurry and flew out the door, feeling rather pissed off that he just threw my beautiful lunch into the trash.

"Please tell me this is your pregnancy hormones right now because you're being ridiculous!" he said, following me out the front door.

Athun was right and I knew it before the words even came out of his mouth, but it was too late. I buckled Olivia into the truck and jumped when I realized Athun was still behind me.

"Athun!"

"Cora, I feel awful. I have no clue what just happened, but the last thing I want to do is upset you. You were completely right. I don't know why I didn't just cook that for you."

I stood there and cried. I couldn't explain why I was crying over Athun throwing my sub away. I felt defeated.

"Come here. Don't let Olivia see you cry," he said, pulling me towards him and wrapping his arms around me. "If you come back inside, I'll take it out of the trash."

"Eww!" I laughed. "No. That's okay. I'll go make something at home. I was just really looking forward to that sub, not to mention how hungry I am. I'll talk to you later," I told him, hoping he would understand I just needed my space.

"Okay," he said, kissing me on my forehead and letting me go.

On my ride home all I could think about was all the running I had been doing. First I ran from Travis and then my parents. Now I run from Weston to Athun and from Athun back to Weston. I needed an outlet of my own, away from Athun and Weston that I wouldn't run away from. I was pretty good at taking care of both of them, cooking meals, cleaning house and laundry. That's when the idea popped into my head that maybe I could go on Craigslist and find someone needing some extra help around their house, like an elderly person.

Elderly person. Sherri! The Golden Years!

I cooked grilled cheese sandwiches with tomato soup for me and Olivia while I looked up visitation hours for Sherri's nursing home. I couldn't find anything on non-related visitors, but certainly if I had Sherri's granddaughter with me, I'd be okay.

****

Dressed. Breakfast in our bellies. Teeth brushed.

"Olivia, Cora has a new adventure for us today. Are you ready?"

"Yeah."

I started feeling nervous as we drove to the nursing home. Should I have asked Weston if this was okay? He said Sherri has Alzheimer's. What if she freaks out when she doesn't recognize me?

"Grammie!" Olivia cheered when we parked.

"Yes, we're going to see if we can visit Grammie today."

"Good morning," the lady at the front smiled. "Hey! I know you, Miss Olivia. Where's your daddy today?"

And to think I was going to lie and say I was a relative.

"He's at work. I'm just her nanny..."

"Oh, well sign your name into the guestbook and write down who you're visiting before you head on down. Olivia knows where to go and if she gets lost, it's your last door on the right," she told me, pointing to the hallway on her left.

"Thank you."

I grabbed Olivia's hand.

"Okay Olivia, you show me the way!"

Olivia slowly walked down the hallway, looking into every open door, but never stopping until we reached the end of the hallway.

"Which door? This one?" I asked, pointing to my left. "Or this one?"

She pointed to the right door.

"You are such a smarty pants!"

Just before I could knock, the door opened and out stepped a woman in pink scrubs.

"Oh, hello," she said, stopping just before she crashed into

Olivia. "I didn't realize Sherri was having visitors today. I'm sorry to tell you this, but I'm afraid she's not having a good day."

And what does that mean exactly?

"Oh...okay," I stuttered, not sure how to explain this to Olivia.

"Lenny!" Olivia squealed when she turned and saw a man standing behind us in the hallway.

"Hello sweetheart. Sounds like your grandmother is a little busy today. Would you like to come on in for some bird watching? I just had them put a feeder outside my window so now...we sit and wait," the man said, grinning down at Olivia.

Olivia looked up at me and I nodded.

"Come on in and I'll give you a tour."

His voice was a touch raspy, but cheery. We waited patiently as the man opened his door and made his way inside. I followed right behind Olivia, wondering what I was getting myself into.

"I'm Lenny and what's your name?" he asked, smiling at me.

It was all I could do not to laugh at Lenny. He was a cute old man with thick black glasses and more wrinkles than a pug. He had white tape with gauze hanging out on his forehead and he was frail looking. If I ever gave him a hug, surely, I would break a bone or two.

"Cora."

"Oh, Maura. Sherri's daughter!"

"No, no. Cora!" I said, a little louder now. "I grew up with Maura."

Lenny just stood there looking pleased and I wondered if he was able to hear anything I had just said.

"Oh, oh. Right there, Olivia. Look! That right there is a cardinal."

"Cardinail," Olivia repeated. Lenny and I both chuckled.

"Close enough," Lenny told her.

"So how is Sherri?" I asked.

"You know Sherri?"

I let out a snicker.

"Sherri was like a second mom to me," I said, trying to speak louder than usual.

"She was? That's so nice. So, you're a family friend?"

"Well, yes. I also watch Olivia."

"That's your job...you mean, full-time?" he asked, confused.

"Yes. We just came to visit Sherri to see how she is doing," I repeated, hoping Lenny would answer my original question.

"Oh. Sherri has good days and bad. Some days she can tell you what her favorite cereal was when she was six. Other days she's fa-la-la. You know, dancing around in her own world."

I nodded my head, letting Lenny know I was listening.

"Do you have any grandchildren?" I asked him.

"Look Olivia! Look!" Lenny bellowed. He pointed out the window again and Olivia followed the direction of his finger with her eyes, practically jumping at his excitement. His love for birds was quite amusing. It was then I realized Lenny and I were not going to be able to carry on a conversation.

"I have grandchildren," he said, continuing to look out the window, "but none that come to visit me. I don't blame them. This place is depressing. We give out candy to trick-or-treaters at Halloween, but my grandkids are older and no great-grandbabies yet."

"Aaaah. Okay. Well, we'll make it a point to visit you then."

"Don't get an old man's hopes up."

"No way! My grandparents have since passed, so if I start visiting you and you like me, I'll let you adopt me. Deal?"

Lenny started beaming, bearing his false teeth. Gosh, he was such a cute old man.

"I was actually thinking of trying to find someone who is in need of help," I said, trying to fulfill my next mission.

"Help? What kind of help?" Lenny appeared puzzled.

"Well, now is a great age to teach Olivia about responsibility and making money."

"And how do you suppose I can help you with that?"

"Well, do you like to eat? Surely Olivia and I can make you whatever you would like. We could be your restaurant!"

"There's a dining hall here."

Oh, right.

"Darn," I said, looking down at the ground.

"Food's terrible."

"It is?" I asked, hoping he'd agree to my request.

"So, you want me to hire a three-year-old as a chef?"

"We can wash any dishes you have, do laundry, mop your floor or grocery shop. You name it, we can do it!"

"Well I'm perfectly capable of doing all those things. I still drive, too."

"You are surely blessed then."

Lenny seemed hesitant about my desire to help him.

"It's just, these days kids don't appreciate the meaning of money. They're fed by a silver spoon or more like a plastic one. Johnny wants twenty dollars so Johnny gets twenty dollars, with no questions asked. I want Olivia to understand that she must work hard for every...single...thing she owns."

"You think she'll understand that at three years old?"

"Almost four and yes, I do. She's very bright!"

"Well, I don't want the police or anyone here telling me I'm slaving a juvenile."

"No, sir, that will never happen." It was all I could do not to laugh at Lenny.

"I do hate to grocery shop. They herd all of the old people onto a bus every Thursday and bring us to that grocery store down the street. Well I don't want to spend all my time there. Gosh do they take forever. The seedless jam or the jam with seeds. Just buy the jam already!"

I couldn't help but chuckle. This guy was a riot!

"Well I noticed on the way in all the cabinets with stuff in them, tissues, toilet paper and even shampoo..."

"Oh, well let me tell you about that," he said, with his hands in the air like he was about to tell me something that would wow me. "Every Tuesday we have bingo here. If you win, you get a ticket. I have to win three games of bingo for a single roll of toilet paper. For Heaven's sake, I don't have time for all of that."

Now I was full on laughing. Boy do I never want to get old.

"So no bingo?"

"No."

"No bus ride?"

"Please no. The workers there, they see our bus pull up and I know what they're thinking, 'oh no, it's the blue hairs again.' I heard last week, Claudette down the hall made a cashier cry over a thirty-cent coupon she forgot to scan. Imagine?"

"Say no more, Lenny. You're in good hands with Olivia and me."

Right away Lenny rattled off a grocery list like he had been thinking about needing each item for quite some time. I took out my phone, using the notes app to write down what he wanted me to buy.

"Olivia and I can bring them to you tomorrow."

"Come over say, ten o'clock," He told me, like he wanted us to visit him again and not just drop off his things.

"That sounds perfect. I will see you then Lenny." I turned

and headed towards the door, realizing Lenny had never given me a tour like he offered. I turned back to find him still smiling. He was accepting of my proposal after all! I got into my truck, grinning from ear to ear. I was on a mission to find some groceries for my new friend Lenny!

I was busy cooking dinner when Weston found me in the kitchen.

"What smells so good?"

"Enchiladas tonight and I think I'll join you and Olivia, if that's okay."

"You and Athun get into a fight?"

"No, he's just been irritating me lately." I paused, thinking about how I couldn't tell Weston that Athun had thrown my deli sandwich into the trash. I was still hiding my pregnancy from him. "He just wants to tell me what I can and can't do. I'm a free bird and I like to do things my way."

"So, you guys a thing now?"

"I guess so. I think he wants more than what I am willing to give him. He deserves a family and I can't give him that."

"I think you need to stop worrying about the future and focus on the present or it'll pass you by."

I smiled at Weston. This was our first genuine conversation we've had in some time. I appreciated his sincerity.

"Thank you for the insight," I said.

"Are you making fun of me?"

"I wouldn't dare."

"What is it you are doing anyway?" Weston asked, looking at the notebook, pen and coupon booklets from Sherri's newspaper subscription that had yet to be cancelled.

"Well, I really don't want to tell you because I have this idea and I'm afraid you're going to say no, but I've never lied to you and I'd rather not start now."

Although I am keeping my pregnancy from you...

"What is it?"

"It's harmless! I promise."

"Out with it, Cora. You are always up to something new."

"Well, I made a new friend today. He's eighty-nine and he would like if we could do his grocery shopping for him."

"And you're worried I will say no. Why?" he asked, confused.

"Because he is going to help me teach Olivia about chores and working to make money."

"You think grocery shopping is a chore?"

"Yes and no. The old man is stubborn and this is just my way in. I think once he sees we are useful, he'll have us doing other things, like cleaning his dishes and such."

"How did you meet this guy?"

"Don't get mad."

"Cora!"

I closed my eyes not wanting to be scolded. I hated being yelled at.

"Sherri's nursing home. I went to visit her."

"And you ended up at another man's residence?"

"I went there...today...while you were at work. He's a really nice old man and Olivia already knew his name. Sherri wasn't having a good day and she wasn't up to having visitors, so when he saw us in the hallway and invited us in, I thought it would be nice to visit with him instead."

"What's his name?"

"Lenny

"Across the hall?"

"Yeah. Do you know him?"

"Yes, I played football with his grandson. He's a very kind man," he said, his tone softening.

"Phew, I thought you were just going to yell at me."

"Well, first of all, I can't remember the last time I actually yelled. Secondly, I am quite surprised you went to see Sherri without letting me know first. Lastly, should you have discussed the idea with me of teaching my daughter about chores and money?"

"Well, when you put it like that...but you need to trust my judgement."

"So, indeed you weren't going to tell me?"

"You would've never agreed to this. My parents made me do chores for money. American children nowadays have no idea what the dollar is worth and I don't want Olivia to be like that. When Olivia gets older, she will come to you and she will ask for twenty or forty dollars to go see a movie with a friend."

"Yes?" he asked, looking at me like I had three heads.

"Well, I want Olivia to know what it took for you to make that money. I want her to understand you had to work for it. If a child never learns how money it made, then it is meaningless to them. They become out of touch with something so vital to their lives."

"You worry an awful lot about the future."

"I planned on leaving my husband for seven years! Now I have half a million dollars to my name and I'm thirty years old. Sometimes it is good to plan for the future," I said, bloating.

"Yeah? What else are you planning?"

Oh no. Did he know? I shook my head in denial. I wasn't ready to tell him I was planning on giving birth in a few months.

"I bother you, don't I?" I asked. "You can just tell me."

"You don't bother me at all."

"Oh yeah, I'm sure you could think of a thing or two."

He sat there pondering and then a smirk drew on his face.

"There it is, something I do that bothers you."

"Every morning, I wake up before you and I'm holding you. When I try to break from your grasp, you pull at me or you won't let go."

"Are you serious right now? Because I want a little companionship, like our good friend Lenny? I'm sorry for making you feel wanted...what a crime!"

"No," he said, cracking up. "You didn't let me finish."

"Please finish."

"Maybe sometimes I would like to be the little spoon."

"Oh stop. Now I know you're messing with me!" I laughed.

"I am not!"

"How am I supposed to turn over and hold you if I'm asleep?"

"I don't know. You asked what you do that bothers me! I'm just being honest."

I couldn't stop cracking up. I think Weston was being serious, but I wasn't quite sure. Then, the thought crossed my mind that I could never snuggle up to Weston. My belly was only growing larger and surely, he'd be able to notice.

We spent the night watching Trolls with Olivia. I had seen it at least a dozen times now, but anything for my beloved Olivia. Besides, I actually really enjoyed the movie. I made us popcorn the old-fashioned way, where I popped kernels on the stove. They both loved it. Then I served us all some ice cream.

"You just might be the most amazing woman I know," Weston said, as I handed him his bowl. He flashed me that all American smile which had me wondering time and time again how he felt about me. Even after my many nights curled up in Athun's arms kissing, I still wanted Weston to want me. Maybe if Weston realized I wasn't always going to be here, his feelings could change.

"Hey, Weston?" I asked when the movie was over. Olivia

was asleep on the couch. She never could make it through an entire movie.

"Yeah?"

"Have you given any thought to what you'll do once I'm gone?"

"What do you mean? Are you leaving?"

"Well surely I can't stay forever."

"Why?"

Because you'll kick me out when you find out I'm pregnant!

"Weston," I said, snickering, "you won't need me when Olivia goes to school."

"Yes I will! When she gets off the bus and I can't be here on time. And the summers! What about the summers?"

"I don't know. You tell me," I said.

"You don't like it here?"

"I do, honestly, but what about when friends come over to play or have sleepovers? I am not Olivia's mother, yet we sleep in the same bed! What do you want me to tell the other moms? Hell, what do you want me to tell Olivia?"

"Look, I have a ton of shit in my head right now that I know I need to work out."

"What does that even have to do with me leaving?"

"Are you leaving?" he asked, sounding exasperated.

"Not now, but someday."

"I just don't understand where all this is coming from."

"Maybe I am caught up with the future, but maybe you should start thinking about it, too."

I got up from the couch and brought our dishes to the sink. I brushed my teeth, changed into my pajamas and laid in bed. I checked my phone and saw there was a message from Athun.

"No dinner duty for me tonight, huh? It was just a deli sandwich."

"I'm hormonal. Sorry. Forgive me?"

I waited a few minutes for Athun to respond.

"You're forgiven. I missed you, though."

"I'll be over tomorrow night," I texted with a kiss face. I shut the light off and rolled over before Weston came in wanting to further our discussion. I just didn't want him to rely on me any more than what he already did. I was taking Olivia to her doctor and dentist appointments. It made me feel uncomfortable, like it was something he should be doing. I especially felt awkward when they referred to me as Olivia's mother. Every other day I was feeling a new set of emotions. Maybe it *was* these damn pregnancy hormones.

CHAPTER TEN

Olivia and I got up and out the door much earlier than usual since we had work to do. We stopped at the store and got Lenny his things, while I explained to Olivia what we would be doing. Olivia had no concept of money, but that would, hopefully, soon change. After checking in at the front desk of the nursing home, we arrived at Lenny's door with one minute to spare. He opened the door before I could even knock.

"Right on time! I like that Cora and hello to you sweet Olivia." He spoke soft and sweet.

"Hi," Olivia said, waving.

"Come on in."

"May I?" I asked, nodding my head towards the kitchen.

"Sure."

"What is all that stuff you have?" he asked.

"The stuff you needed. I know it looks like a lot, but you know the baggers, they put one item per bag."

"Not the young punks. You must've had an old geezer."

I smiled to myself. Lenny was right, the man that bagged my groceries had to have been in his late seventies. *Was that really a thing I never knew? The younger kids pile items into the bags and the elderly don't?*

"You went through all this trouble for a couple quarters?" he asked, shaking his head.

"My biggest reward is that this little girl, in due time, will learn what those two quarters mean."

"Okay, well I hope this big plan you have all works out."

"It will. You'll see," I told him.

"You don't cook?" I asked. "I saw a resident using the oven in the common area."

"Ah, I tried that Meals on Wheels stuff once."

"Any good?"

"Complete garbage."

"We can cook for you. What's your favorite meal that you can't get here?"

"Fiddleheads."

"Fiddle what?"

"Fiddleheads. You never heard of them?"

"I am looking them up right now on my phone, just to make sure you are not pulling my leg."

I looked at him and he was grinning at me.

"This is a plant," I said, smiling.

"An edible one."

"It says here you can only buy them mid-spring."

"Oh, crackerjacks," he grumbled.

"Well I'll figure something out. I'll get you those fiddleheads!"

"You think of something else, a meal, or Oliva and I can make you cookies."

"I'm perfectly content, Cora. I have my microwave and I'm easy. I really don't need to be doted on. I like a visit here and there from the younglings because being cooped up with all these old people is too much sometimes. I have Sherri. I'm okay."

He sat on the chair inside the kitchen and watched us. I'd hand Olivia an item, guess where it goes and I would look at Lenny before Olivia would place it there. Lenny would either nod his head in approval or tell us where he wanted it.

"Well, if you're not able to teach her about money, you sure are teaching her some valuable life skills."

"That's what I'm hoping. You know, after I graduated high school, I heard they took home economics out of the school system. They don't even teach them how to balance a checkbook or how to write a check. These are such basic important life skills that these kids aren't able to learn."

Olivia's favorite part was scooping up all the noisy plastic bags and consolidating them into one bag.

"You should be a teacher," Lenny suggested.

"I don't know what I want to be. I was an accountant and now I'm not so sure I want to go back. I don't miss it at all."

"Now you're a nanny for this little girl."

"Yes, have you met Olivia's father Weston Ekelhart? He played football with your grandson."

"I know the Ekelhart family."

"Weston lost his wife during the delivery of this precious thing. You might have heard."

"Oh, I do remember hearing that. She wasn't from this country."

"Antigua."

Suddenly, there was a knock on the door and before Lenny could even think about getting up, the door swung open and in walked an elderly woman.

"Nancy told me she was here!"

"Sherri," Lenny said, smiling warmly at her.

Sherri? Weston's Sherri? No way!

I was speechless. Sherri had aged quite a bit. Her hair

wasn't completely gray and white, but just about. *Wow...and her clothes*. They were baggy and practically hanging off her. Her bright red lipstick wasn't applied neatly and ran all over around her lips. It immediately made me wonder what my parents looked like. Sherri was only a few years older than them.

"Who are you?" Sherri asked, as if I had just stepped in front of her. I suddenly felt nervous. I had no clue what to expect or how to act around a person with Alzheimer's.

"I told you, Sher, she's the family friend. She watches Olivia for your son."

"You know Weston?" she asked me.

"Well?" Lenny asked, snapping me out of my trance. I knew right then I had to see my parents and soon. "Nancy told me my grandbaby was here," Sherri went on.

Ut oh. Busted.

My eyes followed Sherri as she made her way over to Olivia, pulling her little body in for a hug.

"Who's Nancy?" I asked Lenny, finally able to find my voice.

Or should I say Nosey Nancy?

"The daytime nurse. You better visit with Sherri too whenever you come here."

Yeah yeah yeah.

Before I knew it, Sherri was leading Olivia out the door.

"Woah. Hello, Sherri," I called after her. Sherri stopped in the doorway. "Where are you and Olivia going?" I asked, trying desperately not to step on Sherri's toes, but after all, Olivia was my responsibility at the moment.

"Oh she's fine. We're just going across the hall to my place. The ladies and I made some cookies yesterday and I know Olivia would love some."

"Okay," I said, cautiously. I went to the door, making sure

to leave it open.

"A little girl with no mother. What a shame," I heard Lenny say. I watched Sherri close her door behind her, but I remained in Lenny's doorway.

"So, you and the girl's father?" he questioned.

"No. I think he's still very much in love with his deceased wife. He blames himself because he asked her to come here, to America."

"That kind of guilt can stay with you your entire life."

I nodded my head.

"So, if you think of anything else you need, I'll give you my number and you can just call me anytime." I urged, taking his pen and notepad off his dinette table and jotting down my cellphone number.

"I love clam chowder. Did you see any of that?"

"You do know we're in Iowa. I just moved from Massachusetts, some of the best seafood there."

"Well that's a bit of a culture change."

"I don't miss it one bit. I don't miss the ocean, the fast pace or the windy roads. I ran away back home. This is where I grew up."

"Ran away, huh? Like a fugitive?" The whites in Lenny's eyes widened. Watching Lenny had me chuckling to myself.

"My husband, we've been married for twelve years now. He got mixed up into the bad stuff. We did the whole rehab thing, too many times to count. He started taking money from clients and not doing the work. The town was big, but people talk. I couldn't take it anymore."

He eyed me suspiciously, so I began cleaning up our mess, not wanting to make eye contact.

"Are you going to give me some kind of a lecture right now?" I asked, feeling Lenny's eyes still on me.

"No."

"You want to, you're just biting your tongue."

"No, you seem bright enough to know that when you run away, it doesn't erase the problem. It just leaves it standing there right where you left it."

"I think I'm still heartbroken, but I try not to think about it. I thought he was my soulmate and my best friend. To learn he had a whole other secret life that I knew nothing about. It gives me such a horrible feeling inside."

"I bet it does."

"And if today, someone who could predict the future or someone as powerful as God spoke to me and they said 'Cora, he's done for good this time, no more drugs,' then I would take him back in a heartbeat. I guess that's what hurts the most. I was just waiting, though, for him to be someone he's never going to be. That's why I got far away from him."

"It's such a shame when good people get caught up in that stuff. It's like it just takes ahold of everything in their life."

"I feel so bad I left, so guilty. I'll probably never get over it. I wonder if he's okay and then at times, I think about how much I hate him."

"Love, it's a very powerful emotion."

"Hate is too," I said.

"Well, what are you doing now?" he asked.

"In general or what am I doing standing in your doorway?" I chuckled.

"She's okay."

"I just worry," I told Lenny. Yet another one of my realizations that I cared deeply for this little human named Olivia.

Just then the door opened and Sherri was sending Olivia across the hall with a little bag of cookies in her hand. I half expected her to follow Olivia back into Lenny's residence, but she gave me a smile before closing her door.

Hmmm. I turned to Lenny.

"Come here, sweet girl," Lenny said, smiling at Olivia. I nudged her over to where he sat. "Here's one dollar for helping me with my groceries because Cora here wanted me to give you two quarters, but she would have to drive all around town to find something worth fifty cents that you could buy."

"They would have added up," I chimed in.

"She needs to see instant gratification. Now go take her to that store where everything is a dollar and let her pick something out. That's how she will learn."

"Thank you."

"Don't thank me, thank that store. It will be your new best friend."

"You know, Lenny, I think you're pretty funny."

"I think you're pretty great yourself," he said, winking at me.

"Thanks Lenny. We'll see you tomorrow with your chowder. What time?"

"Noon."

"Okay, have a good day. Don't eat all those cookies!"

"Olivia, wait up!" I told her as I closed Lenny's door. She was already halfway down the hallway bouncing from one foot to the other.

I got into the truck feeling good about my day. I had made Lenny happy and I was teaching Olivia about work ethic. She picked out a tiny plastic doll with her money. It came with an outfit and a hairbrush. She was so excited. Just watching her play with that doll made all my efforts worthwhile.

When we finally arrived home, we had just enough time to make lunch before it was Olivia's naptime. After she was down, I began prepping for dinner. Weston found me the same way he did most days, in the kitchen.

"How'd grocery shopping for Lenny go?"

"He loved it! It wasn't even about the groceries, Weston. His face lit up right when he saw Olivia and I outside his door. Olivia enjoyed herself, too. She's such a good helper. Lenny gave her a dollar for helping me and she bought herself her very own doll with it," I told him proudly. "Sherri even gave her some cookies."

"You did all that work for my daughter?"

"It was nothing."

"What are you working on now?"

"Dinner. It's fried rice for you and Olivia."

"I take it you and Athun made up?"

"We were never really in a fight. I just needed some space."

"You do spend an awful lot of time with him."

"I spend a lot of time with you, Athun and now Lenny. Three men. I must be blessed."

"Men aren't all that bad."

"Not at all. I would take a man over a woman any day. Guys aren't so moody."

"Don't tell that to a feminist."

I laughed, finishing up and saying goodbye to Weston. I had these crazy fantasies in my mind of what I wanted Weston to say or do, but he never did. I wanted him to beg me to stay, to tell me to stop seeing Athun because he was madly in love with me. I was starting to think I was crazy.

"Cora?" Weston asked. *Oh, please say it. Please beg me to stay!*

"Yeah?"

"Will you do something for me?"

Anything!

"What is it?"

"Would you make it a point to visit Sherri next time you're at the nursing home? I get what you're trying to do with this whole Lenny thing, but she's just across the hall and I know she'd love it if you knocked on her door one day because you wanted to visit. She adores Olivia."

"Sure," I replied, trying to hide my disappointment. I closed the door behind me and left.

CHAPTER ELEVEN

I found Athun sitting on the couch, flicking through the channels on the television.

"No apron?"

"Dinner is almost done. I set a meal in the crock-pot before I left for work this morning."

"I can smell it. It smells delicious!"

Athun pulled me down onto him, planting a sweet kiss on my lips.

"What did you do today?" he asked.

"I made an old man happy and a little girl happy."

"Does that mean you're going to make me happy?"

"Depends on what you have in mind..."

"What do you think about moving in here?"

I was taken aback by his question. Surely he was joking.

"Athun..."

"Cora, whatever it is you are going to say, I don't care. I know you're still married. You can continue watching Olivia. We're adults and we can do what we want."

"I just like where I am."

"Living with some other guy?"

"Yes. I don't mind living with Weston and it's easier with Olivia. I like where you and I are, coming here for lunch sometimes and eating dinner here. There's nothing I would want to change."

"So it has nothing to do with Olivia's father?"

"No, not at all," I lied.

"Why don't you ever invite me over then? I've never even seen where you live."

I sighed. Athun was not going to be happy with me.

"Please don't freak out on me, but I don't have my own room. I mean, I share it with Weston."

"What? Why? The house is that small?"

"No, not at all; it's rather large actually."

"Well what then? Surely you don't sleep in the same bed."

I cast my eyes to the floor. Athun abruptly jumped up from the couch, anger surging across his face.

"Is this some kind of sick joke? We hug and kiss every night and then you go home to sleep with him?"

"It's not like that! There's no physical contact between us. I was the one who started it. When I first came here, I just needed someone to be with, but not like that."

"Have you ever kissed?"

"One time. He kissed me and then pushed me away, saying he couldn't."

"I've heard enough," he said, turning and grabbing his jacket off the couch.

"You're leaving? Where are you going?"

"You think I am just going to sit here and share the love of my life?" he shouted. He stomped towards me until he was inches from my face. "You are the love of my life, Cora! I let you go once and I'll let you go again," he said, turning to leave and slamming the door behind him.

I laid down on the couch wondering what the hell had just happened. I couldn't believe how angry he was! *Why was Athun in love with me?* I had absolutely nothing to offer him. I hated to see how upset he was because he had always been such a wonderful friend. I felt so fulfilled before I came here tonight and couldn't understand how I could completely lose that feeling in the matter of minutes.

I went to the front door, waiting for Athun to return. After a few minutes, I wandered to the crock-pot and served myself a bowl of chili. It was amazing! When I was finished, I cleaned up my bowl and returned to the couch. I would wait for Athun to return. Surely he would come back after he cooled off.

I felt a buzzing from my hip area and sat up, realizing I must have fallen asleep. I looked at the time and saw it was just past midnight. I went to the front window, finding Athun hadn't returned yet. *Where could he possibly be?* I felt the buzzing again. I fished my phone from my sweatshirt and looked to see Weston calling.

"Hello?"

"Where are you?" he asked, sounding annoyed.

"I'm at Athun's."

"Well what the hell? Couldn't you have told me you were staying there?"

"What?" I asked, completely caught off guard by his hostility.

"Have some decency! I wake up and you aren't here. Of course I'm going to worry."

I panicked, frantically hitting the red circle button to end the call. I couldn't handle being chastised again tonight.

Wait. What the hell just happened?

I had had it with all this back and forth push and pull rollercoaster of emotions Weston had me on. I got into my truck and flew home to find Weston had gone back to bed. I turned the light on and he instantly sat up, wearing a very frustrated look on his face while rubbing his eyes.

"What is it with us?...with you." I corrected.

"I was worried."

"You and I...are not a thing! You made that very clear the night you kissed me and then pushed me away..."

"This again?"

"You confuse me, Weston. Sometimes I feel like you care about me and then other times I don't feel that way at all."

"That's what you think? That I don't care about you?"

"Yes," I said, louder than what I had intended to.. I was just so frustrated.

"Cora, keep your voice down! I am all sorts of messed up, I told you that. From the moment you knocked on this door, I wanted us, trust me. I knew you had a good heart from when we were kids. You were always such a sweetheart to everyone. I had never looked at you in that way; you were like a little sister to me growing up. I want you so bad, but I don't think I can. You are nothing like her. How could I be in love with two women that are nothing alike? How can I be in love with two women at all? What if I love you more?"

"I can't do this anymore," I said, shaking my head and starting to cry. I turned to leave the bedroom.

"Please don't leave."

I stopped and turned towards Weston again.

"I'm pregnant," I whimpered. I saw the shock spread across his face. "You heard right. I am pregnant. You hate me now, don't you?" I had my back flush against the wall and I closed my eyes. The tears gushed out like a waterfall.

"Athun's baby?"

"No. He's been monitoring me, though. I'm seven

months."

"Whose then?"

"My husband's. When I knocked on your door that day, I was pregnant, but I had no idea. I swear to you I hadn't a clue."

"All of this is so screwed up," he said, laying back down and turning away from me. I slid down the wall and sobbed with my head in my hands. A moment later, I flinched when I felt Weston by my side. To my surprise, he picked me up and brought me to the bed as I wept. He carefully laid me down and then crawled next to me, wrapping his arm around my waist and holding me as I cried. In that moment, I wanted to go back and undo everything I had done in the last seven months.

"Please don't hate me," I whispered. I would be heartbroken if he told me to pack up my belongings and leave. I had watched a dad who had no clue what he was doing, become confident with his daughter.

He seemed so lost when I met him and now, he knew what he wanted and he wanted me. *What if he loved me more?* I understood I could never replace Raina in his heart. If the timing was any different, he would have looked right past me. *Did he still want me, now that I was about to give birth in two months?*

Weston never said a word to me which I was beginning to realize was just a part of who he was. He gave a tremendous amount of thought to anything he said before he spoke and tonight that was exactly what I needed. I hated a lash out like Athun had given me, saying whatever came to the tip of his tongue and then parting ways in anger.

I just told Weston probably the last thing he wanted to hear and here he was still holding on. I tossed and turned all night. I couldn't get comfortable. It seemed like the baby kicked any time I wanted to go to sleep. Tonight, he or she was doing somersaults in my stomach. The morning light started peering through the window and I saw Weston's face. He was sound asleep as I watched him.

Could I picture myself as a stepmom? Of course, Olivia would make it far too easy for me. I couldn't imagine either of them no longer in my life. We were like a family now.

"Weston." Weston stirred a little, but didn't wake up.

"Weston," I said again, a little louder now. He opened his eyes and looked at me.

"What are you doing awake?" he whispered.

"I can't sleep. This baby is having a party in my belly." He took his hand and moved it towards my stomach. I found his sweet gesture to be so incredibly endearing. I grabbed his hand and moved it to where the baby kept kicking. Weston instantly smiled when he felt the baby kick.

"You have such a small belly."

"I know, but it's actually grown a lot in the last month. No more hiding it with oversized sweatshirts."

"So, this is why you haven't gone to see your parents?"

I just stared at him, wanting to kiss him.

"What's your plan, Cora?"

"Adoption. Athun said he would contact the agency and set it up for me."

"Wait, you're going to give your baby away?" he asked, astonished.

"What did you think I was going to do?"

"Become a mother and raise your own child. Maybe you'd even venture back to your husband."

WHAT?

I sat up in bed, appalled by his answer.

"So, you expect me to leave? When?"

"I don't know. Can you just give me some time to wrap my head around all of this?"

I didn't know what he meant, but I wasn't up for a pillow-soaked with tears conversation again, so I let it go.

"Okay."

I watched him stand up, get out of bed and put his pants on. He slid his shirt over his head and looked at me. I went from wanting him, to wanting to punch him, back to wanting him again within minutes. When he was out of the room, I laid down and went back to sleep. Olivia wandered downstairs shortly after and woke me up by climbing into bed. I grabbed her and snuggled her close to me.

"Olivia, we're going to go see Lenny again today. You should tell Lenny to get a cat so it can keep him company."

Olivia lay there smiling at me. She tugged at something behind her back and out popped dolly.

"Does dolly want to come to Lenny's with us, too?"

Olivia nodded her head.

"Okay, but first the tickle monster would like to make an appearance."

Just like the day before, we stopped at the grocery store to buy Lenny his clam chowder. I filled up the biggest container they had before grabbing a small container of chicken noodle soup for Olivia and a salad for me. Then we checked out and drove to Lenny's place. He seemed joyful to see us.

"Chowder will be ready within a minute, okay? This container is still really hot."

"I'll get Sherri. I told her I'd come get her. She loves chowder. No pressure kid, but this better be good. The last time the dining hall had it, it was disgusting. I mean, not even edible."

Oh boy.

Lenny excused himself. After waiting for a few minutes, Olivia and I went to the doorway to find Sherri's door open. We continued to wait patiently for Sherri to appear. Olivia squealed when she saw her grandmother.

"I'm making clam chowder for Lenny and heard that you love it!" I said to Sherri, smiling and backing up so they could both make their way inside.

I maneuvered over to the kitchen counter to grab us some bowls. Olivia followed. I felt rather awkward now, like all eyes were on me. I turned to see both Sherri and Lenny watching me.

Yup, all eyes were on me.

Like yesterday, Lenny sat at the kitchen table and watched Olivia and I as we undid the containers and poured the soup into the bowls. I heard Lenny and Sherri talking about how wonderful and smart Olivia was.

I wanted to ask Sherri a million questions all the way from "do you remember me?" to "why in the world did you leave Weston to be your power of attorney?" since Weston was accurate in saying he gave Sherri the most trouble growing up. When the soup was ready to be served, I had Olivia sprinkle each bowl with oyster crackers.

"Wow," I heard Lenny mumble in between bites.

"Good wow or bad wow?"

"This is by far the best clam chowder I have ever tasted."

I shook my head, convinced he was just saying this to make me feel good.

"I've never told a lie. This is delicious, the best I tell you!"

"What do you think, Sherri?" I asked, as she took spoonful after spoonful.

"Who are you again?" she asked.

I stumbled to answer her, her question throwing me off guard.

"You're that chef on the television show I watch. Yeah, the cute little thing with the white hat and white apron. You made this chowder on your show the other day."

I glanced from Sherri to Lenny, hoping he'd have some input on what to say right about now.

"This is delicious, sweetheart. Do you mind if I take some to my neighbor, Doris? She loves your show!"

"Sure," I smiled, doing all I could to stifle my giggle.

"How about you, Olivia?" I asked, trying to distract Sherri. I already knew Olivia's answer when I peered into her cup to find it was almost gone.

****

"You have something bothering you?" Lenny asked, after Sherri left with the rest of the soup and raving to the passing nurse about how some top well-known chef just cooked her lunch. "You look deep in thought over there."

Wow. How could Lenny tell?

"Yeah, I doubt you want to hear about it, though."

"Try me."

Just then the door opened and Sherri appeared again. No knock this time.

"Olivia, come. I want you to meet my friends down the hall. They'll absolutely love you," she squealed.

"Sherri," I heard a young female's voice call. A nurse stepped in behind Sherri and placed her hands on either side of Sherri's arms. "You know we must knock on another resident's door first."

"She's okay," Lenny smiled. "We were just enjoying some chowder."

"I want the ladies down the hall to see Olivia. They want to meet Olivia."

The nurse looked at me and I looked at Lenny.

"Go on, Olivia," Lenny said. "Your grandmother wants to

show you off."

The nurse extended her hand to Olivia who shied away until her eyes met mine and I nodded to her.

"I'll bring her back after," the nurse told me.

"Thank you."

I watched Sherri's facial expression until they all disappeared out of view. She was overjoyed which of course took a tug or two at my heart strings. I turned my attention back to Lenny only to realize he had been watching me this entire time.

"I'm pregnant," I told him, hoping I wouldn't have to repeat those words any louder than what I just had.

Without a beat, Lenny's lips turned up into a smile.

"Congratulations."

"By my husband."

"Oh, I see why you're carrying such a serious look around then."

"Mmm-hmm."

"Well, you have a few choices then, don't you?"

"I've already decided to give it up for adoption."

Lenny looked back down at his empty bowl.

"You don't agree?" I asked.

"It doesn't matter what I think, my sweet dear. It matters what you feel."

"What do you think?"

"Have you ever regretted one day you have spent with Olivia?"

"No," I said, instantly. "Never."

"Then what makes you think you would ever regret the time spent with one of your own?"

Woah.

I sat there trying to process Lenny's point of view. I had never even thought of it that way. I got up to clean the kitchen.

After a while, I broke the silence.

"I go to the grocery store every day, so if you need anything, I have no problem getting it for you," I reminded him.

"Well, why in the world do you grocery shop every day?"

"Olivia and I enjoy it. Besides, the produce is much fresher this way."

"It's the only reason I still drove."

"Really?"

"Heavens, yes. Otherwise I would've given up driving a long time ago. I didn't want to be a bother to anyone."

"Oh please, it doesn't bother me at all."

"Well, if you enjoy it."

"I do."

"I haven't paid you for the last time you went."

"Let's make a deal. I'll keep track of everything I buy you and when it reaches a hundred dollars, I'll let you know and then you can pay me."

Lenny was never going to go for this idea. He was old fashion. His generation never relied on credit cards and I owe you's.

"I've never met anyone like you, Cora."

"Ditto," I smiled. "Deal?"

"I could use some tea, the yellow box, it starts with an L," he went on, ignoring my idea.

"Caffeinated?"

"Decaf."

"I can do that!"

"And some body soap. It's in a red bottle, old something or other, the green scent."

"Anything else?"

"That's all I can think of. You truly are a wonderful person. I don't understand why you would want to spend your time with an old-timer like me."

Because you boost my confidence and I could really use that right now!

"Because you are great at teaching little girls about working hard," I told him, just before a knock at the door. I opened the door, finding the nurse and Olivia standing there.

"Thank you," I told her before taking Olivia by her hand and closing the door.

"I almost forgot," Lenny said. "Here's another dollar Olivia. Did Cora take you to get something nice yesterday?"

Olivia proudly held up her doll.

"Thank you, Cora and Olivia! I will see you both soon."

When we arrived home, I put Olivia down for a nap and walked back downstairs. I tried to figure out who I wanted to smooth things over with first. I knew how Athun felt, but what I really wanted was to know how Weston felt. I sat on the front porch and thought about what I wanted to say to him. My heart dropped when I saw his truck pull in.

"What are you doing?" he asked as he neared.

"Just tell me what I have to do."

"For what?"

"To live here and to be with you and Olivia. I'll do whatever you want me to."

My bottom lip began to tremble and It was all I could do to hold back my tears.

He shook his head and looked at the ground.

Oh, this isn't good.

"You want me to go? Just tell me the truth."

No, don't tell me the truth!

"Of course I don't. Even today, I'm mad as hell at you, but I'm still the first guy to leave the job site because I can't wait to come home to you. Before you came into our lives, I was the last one to leave. I didn't want to go home to an empty house. I felt like a bad dad to Olivia, always sitting there just staring at each other and trying to figure out what I was going to feed her for dinner or what to say to her. I drank the pain away, woke up with a headache that matched my heartache and did it all over again."

Weston sat next to me on the step now. He grabbed my chin and turned it towards him, wiping my fresh tears and looking into my eyes. "You make parenting a little girl look easy and she isn't even your own. You turned me into a confident father who has bonded with his daughter more than what I could've ever imagined. You are beautiful, inside and out. You do for others more than you do for yourself. I want you all to myself, not Travis, not Athun. Just...mine. I worry you can't give me that."

"What about the baby?" I asked, knowing full well I could give him exactly what he wanted.

"What do you want?"

"Well, Lenny said something to me about regretting the time spent with my baby and I can't imagine ever feeling that way."

"I want what you want."

"I want you to tell me everything is going to be okay. I want you to support my decision to give my baby up for adoption or support my decision to keep it if last minute I change my mind because I'm so fucking moody right now. I want you to love me, but I don't want you to feel that way because that's what I want..."

"If you want this baby, then we'll tell Oliva she's going to be a big sister. If you want to give it up for adoption, I'll back you one hundred percent. Either way scares the shit out of me. I can't go through what I went through again."

"You won't."

"You don't know that, Cora. You have no idea..."

Weston's words were sobering.

Wait a minute…

"So, does this mean you love me?" I asked, scooting closer to him.

"Every last pound of you," he replied, smiling. I couldn't help but laugh since clearly Weston had noticed I gained quite a bit of weight.

Was I always going to have to drag his emotions out of him or were they ever going to come out freely?

"When did you realize your feelings for me were growing deeper?"

"When you talked about leaving. You weren't around much for dinner anymore. I hadn't realized how much of an impact you had on my life until then. If you got in your truck right now and left, well, I'd feel the same way as when I lost Raina."

Wow. I laid my head on his shoulder.

"You need to go see your parents Cora. There's no excuse."

"I know. I will. Tomorrow, okay? I promise. I'll go when you get home."

"I'll just take the day off then."

"No, I need to think about what I want to say. Please. Go to work and as soon as you get home, I'll go."

"Okay," he said. He stared into my eyes, almost as if he was searching for the answers from my soul. I felt exposed. Then he leaned in and my breath hitched in my throat just before his lips were on mine. I felt his arms around me, bringing me closer to him as we both deepened our kiss. My legs began to tremble. Just as I was pouring the last seven months of emotions through my lips, Weston broke our kiss. We were forehead to forehead, smiling foolishly at one another. *Ah, that smile and it's all for me.*

I moved to Weston's lap, laying my head down on his

thigh. I desperately needed to regain my composure. Even my hands were shaking now. I stared out at the front yard realizing that was the most passionate kiss I have ever had. Weston stroked my hair with his warm hand.

Someone pinch me because this can't be real. Weston Ekelhart just told me he loved me.

I closed my eyes. It was almost winter now, but the air was still crisp and the sun was shining bright.

"I want to stay in this moment forever."

CHAPTER TWELVE

My nervous system was a shattered wreck. The truth was, I didn't want to go see my parents. I did, but not like this. When Weston arrived home, he practically had to push me into my truck to leave.

"I can walk to my parents, you know."

"No, there are no sidewalks and it's too cold outside today. You need to drive."

"They might not even be home..."

"They're home!"

I reluctantly put my truck in reverse and backed down the driveway. Before I got to the road, I drove back to Weston and quickly rolled my window down.

"I love you. I really do. My life is just pure chaos and I'm scared as hell to make this right turn out of the driveway right now, but you make me feel like I can do anything...so thank you."

He stepped onto the bar of the truck, leaning in and grabbing my face.

"I love you, too," he said, kissing me softly. "Now go see them."

When I pulled into my parent's driveway, I felt like I was

going to be sick. I waddled up to the door and pushed the doorbell.

"Hi, can I- Cora, is that you?"

"Hi Momma," was all I could get out before I threw myself at her and wrapped my arms around her. There was nothing more rejuvenating than being in my mother's arms.

"Look at you, you're pregnant."

I nodded my head.

"Come inside. I think we have a lot to talk about." She opened the door further and I stepped inside, the familiar smell of my childhood home filling my nostrils.

"Ron," my mother yelled for my dad.

"Coming sweetheart," I heard him say before he appeared in the doorway. It took him a moment to comprehend his pregnant daughter stood before him.

"Cora, this is a surprise." *You have no idea!* I gave him a giant hug and he kissed my cheek.

"Come...sit. Can I get you anything to drink?"

"Water, please," I said and watched my dad grab a water bottle from the refrigerator. I followed my mother to the living room.

I opened the water and took a large gulp. Before I could even start, my mom started her interrogation.

"How far along are you?"

"I'm due January 12th," I replied, nervous they would chastise me for hiding my pregnancy this long.

"Wow. Is Travis excited to be a father?" my mother asked.

"He doesn't know." I watched the confusion etch across their faces.

Here goes.

"The baby is Travis', but I don't want him to know because he's addicted to heroin. He first tried it when he was a teenager, but he was sober when I met him. Anyway, life was good. Happy marriage and then five years in, he relapsed. I found him in our bathroom unconscious."

My mother placed her hand over her mouth. "Oh, honey," my father said, as he placed his hand over mine.

"Anyway, I don't believe in divorce and I knew in the back of my mind that you two would frown upon it, so I stayed. During the last almost eight years now, Travis has relapsed again and again. He's overdosed and they brought him back with Narcan. He's been to detox. My house is empty because he sold everything for drug money. I ran away to see you both, but when I got here, I panicked. I've been staying down the street with Maura's older brother, Weston. I didn't know I was pregnant when I ran away. I know you think I'm a mess right now and probably a big disappointment, but I'm so much happier. The best thing I ever did was run away."

Both my parents were crying now. "Cora, divorce or no divorce, we love you just the same," my mother said.

"Absolutely," my father chimed in. "You tried, honey. You stayed all that time and that's remarkable."

"I tried, Dad. I tried so hard. I fell in love with sober Travis and I fell out of love with addicted Travis. I feel so bad I just left him. I don't even know if he's dead or alive. I feel like a horrible person."

"He called not too long ago," my mother said.

"He did? When?" I asked, surprised.

"Oh, maybe a month ago. Said you two had gotten into a fight and you left. He asked if I had heard from you. When I didn't hear from him again, I figured you went back home. You know I'm not one to pry into your business, but had I known you were living down the street all this time..."

"I know and I'm sorry for that. After I found out I was

pregnant, I definitely couldn't come here."

"Our love is unconditional, Cora. You should know that by now."

"What changed your mind?" my Dad asked.

"Weston. He practically pushed me here."

"Well I'm glad he did. So, what now?"

"Adoption."

My parents both looked utterly shocked.

"That's the last thing I thought you would say! You always loved playing the mom role throughout your childhood with all those dolls you had. You would make a great mother!"

"If Travis ever found out, he could try to get custody of the baby. I would have to go back to Massachusetts."

"Your secret is safe with me."

"And me," my father said.

"I don't know," I said, feeling completely torn.

"You will," my dad said, placing his hand on mine once more.

That night I stayed for dinner. The following night I invited my parents to Weston's house for dinner and they happily accepted. My parents always adored Weston, so conversation flowed throughout the evening. I introduced them to Olivia who played the shy game the first hour into our evening, but when she made it out of her shell, both of my parents enjoyed playing with her. Surely, they would love a grandchild of their own.

Before my parents left that evening, they invited me to church service at the church up the street. I hadn't been for quite some time and now my dad was the full-time pastor there.

I climbed into bed next to Weston that night, eyeing his beauty.

"What?" he asked when he saw me gawking. I giggled.

"Weston?"

"Cora."

"I think I want to call Travis, to see if he's okay. I'm not leaving. I can't...I won't. Maybe I need some closure. I don't know. I just want to call him. Okay?"

"Okay."

"I just don't want you to find out and think I am hiding something." I snuggled up to him and kissed his cheek.

"Do you think we can take our relationship slow?" he asked.

"What do you mean? We're already playing house, Weston. Everywhere I go, people think I am Olivia's mom."

"I'm talking about sex. I don't think I'm ready. It has nothing to do with not wanting you, though, because I do!"

"Look at me, all fat and ugly. There is no way I am letting you see my naked body pregnant, so take all the time you need. Do you want to talk about it?"

"No. I'm hoping I can just figure it out on my own."

"It's okay to move on you know. If you died and Raina was all alone raising Olivia, wouldn't you want Olivia to have a father? For Raina to find love again and be happy?"

"Of course, but my heart feels something completely different from my brain. I know these emotions are simple in your head, but they're so fucking complicated inside mine. I'm trying though...I promise. I want us...so much."

Hands off. I get it.

"Okay," I said, letting it go. I couldn't begin to understand what was in Weston's head or his heart. Travis was dead to me, but he wasn't actually dead, I could still talk to him. At least, I hope he isn't dead. I knew right then I needed to call him. I wanted to make sure he was okay. I still cared about him. I wasn't angry anymore. If anything, I was angry for wasting all those years hoping he would change, but if I had left earlier, I probably wouldn't have ended up on Sherri's doorstep and reuniting with Weston again. If I hadn't met Olivia, I probably would've never gone to the bike trail and run into Athun.

Athun, I think I will write to him to tell him how I feel. I fell asleep in Weston's arms thinking about what I was going to say to Travis and Athun.

****

I invited Weston and Olivia to come to church and they were both happy to join me. My mom saved the first pew for us to sit in with her. Unbeknownst to me, my father planned on introducing me to the congregation. "Stand up and say hello," he said and I obliged. I could feel my cheeks turning red, but my heart was full because it was clear to me that my father was not ashamed of my protruding stomach. I wasn't wearing my wedding ring and I momentarily wondered what my father would tell them.

When the service was over, Weston took Olivia to the refreshments table. I wandered over to my father.

"Great service, Dad."

"Thank you, my sweet Cora."

"Hey, can I ask you something?"

"Anything."

"Weston, well, he and I like each other. I know I'm still married, but it's him I'm a little worried about."

"Oh?"

"He's still in love with his deceased wife, but he wants a relationship with me."

"Sounds like a wound is still open that never fully healed."

"Right."

"Well you still love Travis, don't you?"

"I don't know. I think so, but not in the same way. Weston said his head and his heart feel something completely different. Do you think you could talk to him? He didn't want to talk to me about it."

"Then what makes you think he'll talk to me?"

"You're a guy! Please? You help people by talking to them, don't you?"

"Yes, I suppose so," he said, still not convinced.

"Please?"

"I can try, but I'm not sure what good it'll do."

"Thank you," I said, kissing him on the cheek.

"I enjoyed your service, Ron," Weston said from behind me. I turned to see Weston and Olivia, with cookie crumbs all over her face. I bent down to her level.

"Ah, I see you got into a cookie, Olivia. How was it?"

"Good. I got one for you, too," she said, pulling a cookie wrapped inside a napkin out of her coat pocket. She was so darn precious.

"Wow, you are so thoughtful! I better eat it in the back of the church so we don't make a mess up here." I grabbed her hand and we headed down the center aisle.

We said our goodbyes to my parents and left the church.

"Thank you for coming with me," I said to Weston and Olivia when we got into the truck. I looked at Weston, hoping he enjoyed our new little family as much as I did.

When we arrived home, I didn't follow Weston and Olivia inside. Instead, I hung back, telling them I was going to make a phone call. I ran through my contacts, calling the number that's been blocked for so long.

"Cora," I heard Travis say on the second ring.

"Hi," I breathed. My heart began pounding faster.

"Where are you?" he asked.

"Does it matter?"

"When are you coming home?"

"Travis..."

"You're not coming back home, are you?"

"No," I just about whispered. I didn't want this phone call to be a fighting match.

"You just left. I've thought about you so many times," he said.

"I know and I'm sorry. If I didn't lose you, I was going to lose me."

Silence stretched through the line and I could only imagine the sound I was hearing was Travis crying.

"I'm sorry about the truck and the camper. I'll return both. I do miss my car."

I heard Travis snicker on the other end.

"What?" I asked.

"I traded your car to the neighbor a few houses down, you know, that old guy with all that junk in his front yard."

"He's driving my car?" I asked, confused.

"Yeah. I couldn't drive your car, Cora. It drove me mental! I bet it still smells like you..."

"Well how'd you sell him my car? It's in my name."

"I just traded it. He didn't seem to care. It was a serious upgrade from the hunk of junk he gave me in return."

I laughed, picturing Travis driving around town in a rusty old beater. The silence grew again. I had no clue what to say.

"I should tell you my mom moved in."

"She did? When? Why?"

"A week after you left I just had this feeling you were never coming back. I called her one night and broke down as I told her everything that had gone on. She packed up her life and moved out here to help get me back on track. She found out shortly after she's sick with cancer. It's spread everywhere in her body. She's with in-home hospice care now."

"Oh my gosh. I am so sorry, Travis. How long do they think she has?"

"Days now."

"Oh no," I said, mentally kicking myself for neglecting this part of my life for so long.

"Can I talk to her?"

"I'm afraid it's too late. She's on morphine and she's just so out of it. She's still breathing, but she's not really there."

"So, if I did talk to her, she wouldn't even know it was me?"

"No. She's like a vegetable, lying in bed right now waiting to die. It's so sad. I want to be there by her side, holding her hand until her last breath, but it's so incredibly hard to see her like this."

"I can imagine."

"The nurse just walked in, so I have to go."

"Okay."

"Thank you for calling. It was nice hearing your voice, to know you're okay."

"I guess it was nice hearing your voice, too."

"Can I call you sometime?" Travis asked.

"Yes. I'd like that."

"Okay."

I hung up hoping that phone call would've given me closure, but instead, it opened up a whole new set of emotions. I wanted to be there for Travis during the last days before his mother passed. Hell, I wanted to be there holding her hand right now. She was such a fun-loving mother, full of personality. Whenever she came to town, we would leave Travis at home and go galivanting throughout downtown Plymouth looking at all the trinkets inside each gift shop. She dazzled anyone she spoke to with her big smile and bright blue eyes. I missed her.

I wondered when I would hear from Travis again as I made my way inside.

"Hey, everything okay?" Weston asked, as I slipped off my shoes. He was making lunch.

"I just talked to Travis."

"Yeah?"

"My mother-in-law is dying of cancer," I could barely get out as I sat at the counter. Weston was by my side in a heartbeat.

"I'm so sorry."

"This is awful. I'm not even there. They put her on morphine so she's not in any pain. Travis said I can't talk to her because she's not coherent enough to even know who I am."

"That means she'll probably go soon."

"Travis said it's a matter of days. He's there with her, in our house."

"I think that's the best way to go, not in some hospital, but at home surrounded by people that love you," he said.

Weston's words made me cry even more, knowing I should be one of those surrounding her. We were very fond of each other from day one. I heard people talk all the time about how nasty their mother-in-law was. I adored mine.

"Are you going to go back?" he asked.

"I don't know. I think I'm going to go for a ride. I'll be back later. Okay?"

"Aren't you hungry? I made you a sandwich."

"I'll take it to go." I got off the barstool and headed to our bedroom to grab a notebook and pencil. When I was sad, I wrote it all out onto a white lined piece of paper, which usually made me feel better. When I returned to the kitchen, Weston had a sandwich all wrapped up for me to go.

"Thanks," I said and kissed him on the cheek.

"Should I be worried about you?"

"No. I'm just really sad right now and want to be alone."

"Okay."

I jumped into the truck and drove. After driving around trying to figure out where I wanted to park, I found myself at the bike trail. For some reason, this place is a comfort zone for me now. I sat at the picnic table behind my truck. As I ate my sandwich and drank my water, I thought about carrying Lillian's grandchild and how she would never get to meet him or her. She would leave earth not even knowing she was going to be a grandmother.

If I kept this baby, Travis would never know he is a father. *Could I live with that guilt? Was that my choice to make?* I couldn't think about it anymore. It made me feel like a monster.

I decided I would write a letter to Athun and stick it in his mailbox. I wanted him to be a part of my life, but not the way he wanted.

Athun,

I'm sorry. Can we start over? I want a re-do from the day I first saw you on the bike path. I never should've led you on. I was hurt and broken. Truthfully, you taught me how to feel again. You cared about me and showed me love when I didn't even care about myself. If I could go back all the way to high school and do it all over again, I never would've left. I should've stayed, maybe we could've been something then. Now, I look at you and I know you belong with someone better than me, who doesn't carry around a daily mountain of baggage.

You want a wife and a family and that is not where my head is at. I don't want to lie to you. I've fallen in love with Olivia's father, Weston. I didn't want to, but I did. I can't imagine

you understand what that means. I've known him for as far back as my memory goes and he's always been a safe place for me.

Anyway, I want you to be a part of my life. I hate this fighting. I wish we could go back to the days we drove around with a beer in between our legs, underage and freaking out when we drove by a cop. Getting lost in that cornfield late at night and literally thinking we were going to be stuck out there until the sun came up.

I love you Athun. Can we just go back in time? You're the best friend anyone could ever ask for.

-Cora

I scanned my surroundings knowing that Athun came here every day. My heart skipped a beat as I stood up to throw my trash away and was able to get a better look at the parking lot. I didn't see Athun's car. I got back into the truck and headed over to his house.

When I stopped at his mailbox, I couldn't reach it through the window. I tried to stretch, but it was no use. My stomach was too big. I pulled up the street a little bit to open my door and hopped out. I was hoping no neighbors were watching me as I was starting to look rather suspicious.

"What are you doing?" I heard a voice say. When I looked up, I saw Athun standing on his front step with his hands on his hips.

"Just leaving you something."

"I'm right here. You can bring it to me."

"Do I have to?" I asked, opening his mailbox and placing the note inside. I let my hand rest there waiting for Athun's answer.

"Impossible woman," he said, walking through his front

lawn until he reached me. He tugged at my hand that was still holding the letter.

"What's this?"

"I just wanted to write to you. I know we didn't end things too nicely the other night. You were mad, really mad and I don't want you to yell at me like that again, so I figured if I just left this in your mailbox..."

"I'm sorry."

"That's what my letter says, that I'm sorry."

"You want to come inside?" he asked.

"So I can watch you read my letter? No. That's weird!"

"Okay, I'll just read it here then," he said, snatching it out of my hand.

"Athun," he read.

"You're reading it out loud? No, stop, stop, stop! This is so awkward, I'm leaving. Call me when you want to." I turned to leave.

"Go park in my driveway, you brat."

"Can you stop reading my letter then? I'll come inside."

"Okay."

I parked in his driveway, smiling to myself. He was cheering me up without even trying.

"You're in love with that guy? I knew it!"

"You said you'd stop reading my letter..."

"No I didn't. I just read the whole thing. I remember we got stuck in that cornfield, you started crying."

"Yeah, which made you laugh so hard you were crying too, you jerk!"

"Oh man, telling me you were going to call your parents to tell them you couldn't find your way out of corn." He started cracking up all over again, just like that day. I shook my head at him. After a moment, his smiled disappeared.

"About the other night, I'm sorry I yelled at you, I really am. I felt so bad after I did."

"Where did you go? I waited for you."

"I know. I drove around and when I came back home, you were still here, but I didn't want to see you or talk to you."

Ouch!

"That makes me so sad," I admitted.

"It makes me so sad you don't see me the way I see you."

"I wanted to change that. I tried to change it. I did want to have sex with you that night you weirdly knew I was pregnant. I think you're really sexy. I don't know what's wrong with me."

"You just like him more."

"I guess so. Is that going to be a problem for us?"

"For my penis."

"Shut up," I said, smacking his arm.

"Cora, if you're happy, I'm happy."

"I'm as happy as I can be," I replied, finding my way over to Athun and giving him a side hug. "I'm starving. Do you have anything to eat?"

"I was just going to make nachos."

"Yes!" I said, louder than what I intended, which made Athun crack up laughing. We headed to the kitchen. I watched as he wandered about through his kitchen pulling out everything to make ultimate nachos. He really was a catch, just not my kind of fish.

"You want to watch a movie?" he asked.

"Can we please do a chick flick? I'm begging! I'm hormonal."

"Well, I wouldn't want to mess with hormones."

"Thank you," I squealed with delight.

"You have definitely gotten bigger since I last saw you."

"Athun, that was just a few days ago. It's not possible!"

"I'm telling you, you look bigger," he said, smiling.

"Could you not? I already feel like a whale."

"Oh stop, you look beautiful. Still taking your prenatal every day?"

"Yes, Doctor."

"Don't get cute with me. After all, you are MY patient," he said, taking the plate of nachos out of the microwave and heading towards the living room. I grabbed us waters and followed.

"Here," he said, handing me the remote. "I don't want to pick the wrong chick flick."

I landed on the movie Safe Haven. It looked like a total love story. We dove into our nachos. They were delicious! When I was done eating, I scooted closer to Athun. He put his arm around me and I gladly accepted it. I felt like we were right back in high school again.

When the movie was over, Athun offered to cook me dinner, but I knew I had to get home to Weston and Olivia. I didn't want Weston to think my heart was not in our relationship.

"Is this how it's always going to be? I can't cook dinner for you anymore?"

"No, but if I want to be a part of Weston's family, then I should probably start acting like I am and eating dinner with them like a family does."

"Oh, okay, Cora."

"Oh, please, don't give me that. I see you every day on the bike trail. When it rains or if it's cold, I'll come here and we can still eat lunch together, you big baby! That's five days a week you get to see me."

"For a half hour? Not even, whoop de doo."

I shook my head at him smiling.

"I'll come over every Sunday afternoon and we can do whatever you want. Is that better?"

"Whatever I want?"

"No, not that," I said, laughing. I gave him a hug goodbye. "I'm sorry I can't be who you want me to be, I really am. They say you should marry your best friend. I guess I should've listened."

"They also say everything happens for a reason," he said, hugging me back and holding me. I just let him hold me there in the entryway. After a few minutes, he kissed me on the forehead and said goodbye.

On my way home, I called Weston.

"Hello?" he answered.

"Hey! Do you want me to stop and grab some dinner for us?"

"No. I saw those chicken sausages in the fridge, so I hope you don't mind I used them. I'm cooking up a meal and I think you'll like it!"

"Okay, great! Is Olivia up from her nap yet?"

"Oh yeah, she's helping me with dinner."

"Awesome! I'll be home soon."

"Okay, bye."

"Bye."

When I walked through the door, a sweet savory smell hit my nostrils.

"That smells amazing," I said, going to Olivia and kissing her on the cheek. "Are you helping Daddy cook?"

"Yes, it's super good," she replied with a big smile. She loved being a daddy's girl.

"I'll set the table," I said, grabbing some plates from the cabinet.

"So, where'd you go?"

"To the bike trail and then to see Athun."

"I want to go with you," Olivia said.

"I already went, when you were sleeping. I'm sorry.

Tomorrow?"

"Yay," she cheered. I grabbed some silverware, eyeing Weston suspiciously. I knew he wouldn't be pleased I was upset and went running to Athun. Well, that's not how it went, but that is how Weston would see it. I stopped and looked at him, but he wouldn't look at me.

I folded some napkins and got us all some water. I picked Olivia up and put her in her chair as Weston brought dinner to the table.

"Olivia, this looks so good," I said, clapping my hands as Weston served our plates. Olivia was clapping with excitement now, too.

"Oh, my word, this is amazing! How'd you make this sauce?" I asked.

"Half honey, half vinegar," Weston replied.

"You just made it up? No recipe?"

"Yeah. I tried it and I liked it..."

"That's awesome! I wish I could do that."

I watched Olivia as I ate my meal. Just looking at her brought warmth to my heart. I couldn't believe how such a little person could change my life in such a big way. I couldn't imagine going one day being completely miserable with her in my life. She could take every single one of my frowns and turn them upside down without even trying.

"So, any more thoughts on going back to Massachusetts?"

"Yes. I decided I'm not going to go. I just can't. If I did, I could risk losing all this," I answered, running my hand through the air. "I'd risk losing both of you. These past few months have made me realize that what I have right now and being here with you guys is exactly what I've always wanted."

Weston grabbed the back of my head and brought me to him, kissing me on the lips.

"I love you," he said, which was exactly what I needed to hear right now.

"I love you, too."

I pointed to Weston to look at Olivia. She was staring at us, smiling.

"You like when I kiss Cora?"

Olivia nodded her head.

"I love you too, little girl," he told her.

"I love you and you," Olivia said, pointing to the both of us.

"And I love you, too!" I said to Olivia.

After we cleaned up dinner, we ate some ice cream.

"You guys have any board games here?"

"If we did, they'd be downstairs," Weston replied. We ventured downstairs to this massive closet full of games and trophies.

"Are these your trophies?"

"I think, some of them at least. Probably my brother's, too."

"I remember you loved hockey."

"I love every sport. It was my dad who loved hockey."

"Oh, that explains it. Hey, here's Go Fish and a matching game. It says age four and up, but you catch on pretty quickly, Olivia. I bet you would love these!"

We played the night away. When we were sick of playing Go Fish and matching, I ventured back down to the closet and brought up Candy Land. Olivia loved Candy Land. When it was time for Olivia to go to bed, we both tucked her in. She was one happy little girl.

"Weston?" I said heading back down the stairs.

"Cora."

"Can I paint Olivia's walls and decorate her room so it's a little more girly? I mean, it looks like a guest bedroom."

"It is a guest bedroom."

"Well now it's not, right?"

"I guess."

"What do you mean you guess? I saw you moved your clothes in," I said, snickering. "You're here every night. We live together. We're a family. Is that a hard reality for you?"

"Not at all," he replied, kissing me.

"Am I not what you had in mind?" I asked, pointing to my growing basketball of a belly.

"Stop," he said, smiling at me and hushing me with another kiss. He walked me backwards and towards the bedroom, breaking our kiss to bring my shirt up over my head. I mirrored his actions, running my hand along his abs. He was a mighty fine sight to see.

He undid my bra and I knew just what he wanted. *Oh no, do I want this? Yes. No, I'm pregnant and huge. I'm so turned on right now, though. I don't want him to see my body*. I took one look into his eyes and I knew I wanted this just as much as he did.

"Are you sure?" I asked.

"Yes," he replied.

We made love that night, totally unexpected and unbelievably amazing. I had never been with anyone but Travis. I haven't had sex like that in so long. It wasn't sex just for pleasure, it was sex for the simplicity of being in love with each other. It was like a breath of fresh air.

I fell asleep to the beating of Weston's heart as I laid on his chest.

When we woke in the morning to Weston's alarm, I felt different, but I couldn't put my finger on it. I looked at Weston with a goofy look on my face.

"Go back to sleep," he mumbled. "What are you smiling about so early in the morning, anyway?"

"You."

"What about me?"

"I don't know. You tell me you want to take things slow and then bam."

"I know. Sorry..."

"Please, don't apologize. That was amazing last night!"

"What about you? Mrs. I'm Fat and Ashamed of My Body."

"Technically, the lights were off."

We both laughed. Then Weston slipped out of bed to get dressed.

"It just felt right," he said, leaning down to kiss me and then left the room.

I knew exactly what Weston meant. What I was doing was so wrong. After all, I was still married, but something about us just felt so right.

Shortly after Weston left, I heard my phone ringing. It was Travis.

"Travis?"

"She's gone, Cora. She's gone!"

"I'm so sorry." I started crying and I could hear him crying too.

"Just happened so fast," he breathed.

"I can't believe it. I'm so sad I didn't get to say goodbye."

"I have no idea what to do now. I'm clueless with this stuff..."

"Call everyone in your family, aunts, uncles and cousins. Write an obituary and call a funeral home. They'll walk you through everything."

"Will you help me write the obituary?"

"Of course."

"How do I know if she had anything?"

"What do you mean? A will? Money?"

"Yeah."

"She should've had a will. I mean, most people do. She moved out of her apartment and brought everything to our house?"

"Yeah."

"Look around then. It has to be with her stuff."

"I wish you were here."

"I know. I'm sorry."

"Do you think you'll come back for her funeral?"

"I don't know," I lied. I had already made up my mind I wasn't going back.

"I'm clean you know. I've been clean since you left."

"Really? How do you feel?"

"So much better. I couldn't do it anymore. Look at everything I lost, including you."

"I'm so sorry she had to find out the way she did."

"I'm not. If you hadn't left, she would've died in Florida and all alone."

"Everything happens for a reason."

"I promised her I would stay clean. I'll never touch that shit again."

"I hope you stay true to your word."

"If I continue to stay clean, will you come back home?"

No.

"I don't know."

"The longest I went was nine months. I'm almost there again. What if I go a year? Two years? Will you come back then?"

No!

"I don't know, Travis. Can we talk about this after everything settles? Let's work on the obituary and the funeral arrangements. Okay?"

"Okay."

"I have to go. The little girl I watch is here."

"Are you nannying again?"

"Yes and I love it! I thought I loved accounting, but I don't know. I don't think I want to do that anymore."

"Wow, but you loved the money!"

No, but you did!

"I thought I did, but now I love happiness more."

"Ouch."

"No, that wasn't a dig at you. I'm saying being around children makes me far happier than crunching numbers."

"I could see that."

"I'll talk to you later. Okay?"

"Okay. 'Bye."

I hung up and said good morning to Olivia, pulling her into bed and kissing her.

"The baby just kicked! Do you want to feel it?"

Olivia nodded her head smiling. I placed her hand on my stomach and we waited for the baby to kick.

"Did you feel that?"

"Yes."

"He or she is saying good morning."

We laid there snuggling as I thought about Travis. I only hoped someone from his family would be there for him. His father passed years earlier from a heart attack. He was in his wood shop, his favorite place to be. When Lillian hadn't seen him in a few hours, she went out to look for him, only to find him dead on the floor.

Travis was an only child. He had less than a handful of cousins. I had met a few aunts and uncles from either side. I couldn't even tell you who was who, though. I felt bad for him. He truly was alone. *Why would he ask me about her will?* It seemed like all anyone ever wanted when someone died was to find out their inheritance, if they had any. Maybe he needed money for the funeral. I would ask and somehow send him money if I needed to.

"Let's start our day, pretty girl," I said, getting out of bed and tugging at Olivia's hand. "What should we do today?"

"Moosey! Moosey!"

"Oh, you're adding a y to the end of your favorite dog's name now, huh?"

"Moosey," she squealed again, giggling.

"You are a creature of habit, aren't you?"

"Creature?" she asked, scrunching up her nose at the new vocabulary word.

"Yes. A person, a girl...a creature."

"Creature," she repeated in her adorable voice.

"Come."

Olivia and I ate breakfast and then I gave her a bath. I called Lenny before we left for the bike trail, hoping to see if Olivia or I could do anything for him this week, but he didn't answer. I pushed Olivia in a stroller along the bike trail as she was too heavy for me to pick up. After about a mile, I was starting to get tired and turned around.

"Moosey?" Olivia asked.

"I know, no sign of him yet, huh? I'll see if they are coming today." I shot Athun a text, "Olivia is on the lookout for Moose, but he's not at the bike trail. Where is he?" I wrote with a smiley face. When we arrived back to the truck, my phone went off. It was a text from Athun, "Emergency caesarian today, key is under my mat."

"Moosey is at home. Do you want to go see him?" I asked Olivia.

"Yay," she cheered. We stopped at the grocery store and I filled up two salad containers. The further on into my pregnancy, the more I piled into the container. I felt like I was always hungry and I craved peanut butter. Peanut butter cookies, peanut butter shake, peanut butter on graham crackers or hell, I would just eat it out of the jar.

Olivia and I stopped by Athun's and ate our lunch, then we took Moose for a walk. I snapped a picture of little Olivia walking big Moose and sent it to Athun. We returned Moose, locking up Athun's house and I knew just what I needed to do…write my mother-in-law's obituary. I would enjoy writing about such a wonderful woman.

I sat at the kitchen counter after I put Olivia down for her nap. I opened my laptop and pictured my mother-in-law's face.

Lillian Ann Cavanaugh died peacefully in her son's home on November 2, 2017 at the age of fifty after a short battle with cancer. She was born on December 14, 1967, in Colorado Springs, Colorado.

Lillian's personality could light up a dark room. She could stop the rain and pull out rays of sunshine with just one conversation. Her captivating aura made everyone around her feel loved. She had a knack for making everyone she talked to feel special. She made friends everywhere she went and has touched the lives of so many people.

Lillian is predeceased by her husband, Travis Cavanaugh Sr. Lillian will be lovingly remembered by her son, Travis Cavanaugh and his wife, Cora Cavanaugh of Massachusetts.

I sent the obituary to Travis via e-mail, telling him he needed to finish it with the names of her siblings and funeral arrangement information. I called Lenny again, but there was still no answer.

I started dinner and when Weston came home, I left to check on Lenny. Something just didn't seem right.

"Can I help you?" the receptionist asked.

"I'm here to see Lenny."

"And you are?"

"Just a friend. I've called him a couple times today, but he didn't answer. It's not like him, so I'm worried."

"What's your name?"

"Cora."

Just then I saw a nurse that I knew would remember me. She always said hi to Olivia. I waited until we made eye contact until I flagged her down.

"Hi. It's Lenny, he's not answering my phone calls..."

She took me off to the side and spoke quietly.

"Lenny had a bad fall over the weekend and had to stay in the hospital a couple of days. He just got discharged this morning and needs to rest. How about you call him in a week or so, okay?"

"I usually help him with meals and stuff...he might need me."

"His kids are going to be in and out bringing him food and we're here, too. He's okay, so don't worry," she said with a smile.

"Okay," I said, not persuaded enough that he was going to be properly cared for. He hardly talked about his children. I stepped backwards creating more space between us, but I was not convinced I was ready to leave.

"Have a nice day."

"You too," I said over my shoulder and returned home.

"So, is Lenny okay?" Weston asked, as I walked through the door.

"No. I knew something was up! He fell over the weekend and spent a couple of days in the hospital. The nurse there wouldn't let me see him. I'm so frustrated!"

"Just give it a week."

"That's what she told me. I'll give it one week and then I'm going back there!"

"You're really fond of this old man, huh?"

"I just want to make sure he is okay. I don't have a grandfather anymore and he reminds me so much of mine. He even looks like him. He does this thing my grandfather used to do, where he would just listen to me talk and not ever say anything. I would have to ask him his opinion because even though I knew he had one, he'd never say it."

"Sounds like a smart man. You never give a woman your opinion unless they ask for it."

CHAPTER THIRTEEN

A week later I went to visit Lenny. He hadn't called me needing anything since I dropped off his stuff last, so I just planned on checking in to see how he was doing. When his door swung open, I was met by a man about my age, maybe a little older, with dark blue eyes and sandy brown hair.

"Hi," I said, confused.

"Hi."

"Who are you?" I blurted out.

"Shouldn't I be asking you that?" he sneered.

"Sorry, I'm a friend of Lenny's. My name is Cora. I come here every week to take care of him. I bring lunch or grocery shop, whatever he needs."

"Hi Cora. I've heard the name. I'm Lenny's grandson, Ben."

He's heard of me?

"Nice to meet you, Ben. So, is Lenny okay?"

"No."

"What do you mean?" I asked, trying hard not to get emotional. Ben closed the door behind him and stepped out into the hallway. I crossed my arms.

"He's sick."

"Sick sick or just sick?"

"Sick sick with cancer and he's known for some time," he replied, shaking his head.

Oh no, not another death.

"How bad?"

"He's refusing treatment."

"Why?"

"Some bullshit about having lived a fantastic life and he's ready to go."

"How long?"

"The doctors aren't sure. It could be months or if he gets treatment, years. They really don't know."

"Oh my gosh! And he knew?" I suddenly felt betrayed. I could just imagine how Ben feels.

"My dad said he kept it from us because he knew we would want him to get help and he doesn't want any."

"Wow! I'm so sorry."

"I mean, my grandfather is right, he has had a wonderful life. I think he wants to be with his wife again."

"When did she pass?"

"About eight years ago...breast cancer."

"I'm so sorry. That's how one of my grandmothers passed also. My other to colon cancer."

"Catches up with all of us."

"Well, can I see him?"

"I guess. I'll go ask my dad. He's inside with him now. So, how did you meet my grandfather?"

"Well, it's kind of weird, but the lady across the hall...well, I nanny for her granddaughter. I think your grandfather was looking for a little companionship."

"You and my grandfather?" he asked, scratching his head and looking at my pregnant belly.

"No, no, gosh no! We were here visiting his neighbor and she wasn't available, so your grandfather invited us in. The little girl I watch, you might know her father, Weston Ekelhart. Anyway, I figured I would teach his daughter Olivia about working and helping people which is how we began caring for Lenny."

"Well, that is kind of weird. How do you know Weston?"

"I grew up down the street from him."

"His wife died, right?"

"Yes, giving birth to his little girl. So sad."

"I played hockey with him."

I nodded my head, unsure of what to say.

"So...I can come back another day..."

"I'll go see if my gramps is up for a visit. I'll be right back," he said, changing his tone. He opened the door and shut it before I could even reply. Moments later, he was bringing me inside. He led me down the hall to Lenny's bedroom. Lenny was sitting up in bed, smiling when I entered the room.

"Dad, this is Cora. She brings Grandpa meals, I guess. Cora, this is my dad, Dane."

"She's a beautiful thing," Lenny announced, smiling broadly.

"Nice to meet you," I said, shaking Dane's hand and sitting on the edge of the bed next to Lenny. I took one look at him and wanted to weep. Just a week ago, he was up walking around and now he looked pale and more fragile as he sat in bed. I grabbed his hand, holding back the tears.

"Can I bring you anything?" I asked him.

"That chowder.. Do you remember? And some oatmeal raison cookies."

"Of course! Tomorrow?"

"Tomorrow."

"Okay, I'll bring Olivia. She's been asking for you," I said, rubbing his hand affectionately. He smiled. I looked over at Lenny's son and grandson who appeared rather confused by my interaction with Lenny.

"I better go. I left my dinner in the oven. I'll see you tomorrow," I told him, cheerfully. I was relieved I got to see Lenny. I didn't realize how much I cared about him until now. I couldn't believe he was dying of cancer. *What was it with everyone around me and cancer? I hated the C word.* When I parked the truck back home, my cellphone rang. It was Travis again.

"Hi Travis."

"I got your e-mail, thank you. It's perfect!"

"Well it's not finished yet, but it's a start."

"I'm already on it. The wake is in a couple of days and then the funeral is the morning after. Can you get back to town by then?"

I let out a long sigh. "Travis..."

"Why, why won't you come home? Your mother-in-law just died! She loved you like her own daughter!" he growled.

"I know." I started crying. I already felt guilty, let alone hearing it from Travis' own mouth.

"Why then?"

"I don't trust myself."

"What's that supposed to mean?"

"I don't trust myself with you. If I come home, I might never leave again."

"You should stay! I am your goddamn husband!" he yelled.

"That means nothing anymore. A marriage is not what you and I have. You are my biggest weakness. I would do anything for you. There's too much that's broken for anything to be fixed. Can't you see that?"

The line went dead. I pulled the phone away from my ear

and looked at it. He had hung up on me. He had never done that before. I suddenly feared he would relapse. With his mother just dying and now realizing I was never coming back home. *Oh no, what did I just do?* I checked my face in the mirror. It was red and blotchy. I re-applied my makeup and walked inside.

"Hey! Were you going to eat without me?" I asked, grinning as I saw Weston setting the table.

"Not at all," he answered, smirking. "Hey, Ben just called me fishing for information about you."

"What?"

"Yeah. I guess you saw him at Lenny's?"

"Yeah. I think he thinks his grandfather is my sugar daddy or something."

Weston just about spit out the entire amount of water he had just sipped from his glass. I jumped back in shock.

"What?" I asked.

"I don't think he thinks that at all."

"Why? What did he want to know?"

"If you were available."

"I'm not bringing him food, too! He can make his own damn lunch!"

"No, no, no," he said, shaking his head and laughing. "He wanted to know if you were single because he was interested in you."

"What?" I practically shouted. "I'm pregnant by another man's baby! What the hell would he want me for?"

"Hey!" Weston said.

"What?"

"I want you and that's not my baby you're carrying..."

"I know. It feels like it is, though. It doesn't feel like I'm carrying Travis' baby, probably because he doesn't know he's about to be a father." I poured some soup into my bowl. "So, what'd you tell him?"

"The truth...that you were taken."

"You told him we were dating?"

"Yeah."

"Wow! I'm surprised..."

"Why?"

"I don't know. Aren't you ashamed of me? I'm married and this whole baby thing."

"It's none of anybody's business."

"Did Ben ask?"

"He asked me what your story was."

"What did you tell him?"

"I bought my stepmother's house and you live here with me; that you're my girlfriend."

"That's it?"

"Yeah. The rest is none of his business. You want me to tell him your life story? It's not mine to tell, but am I ashamed? Not at all. Everyone has a past. You know mine. I never finished high school. I fell into the wrong crowd and cheated on just about every girlfriend I had until I met Raina. People change! I know I have."

Wow.

"Well, what's Ben's story then? He's rather good looking. I'm sure he could find someone a little less pregnant," I chuckled.

"Actually, I just heard his longtime girlfriend dumped him right after he popped the question."

"What? I thought that only happened in the movies..."

"Apparently not."

Well, everybody did have their own story. Didn't they?

****

I took Olivia to the grocery store to buy Lenny's lunch, but when I went to give it to him, I was told he was getting a sponge bath so Olivia and I didn't dare disturb him. Instead, we left it with the front desk.

I was now in the last month of my pregnancy and I wondered how much bigger I could possibly get. I could no longer see my lady business or my toes and I definitely couldn't tie my own shoes. It was hard to pick something up off the floor and I missed being able to hold Olivia close.

It wasn't long after that that I started feeling cramping in my lower stomach. I had just put Olivia down for a nap and when I went to the bathroom, I noticed this weird brownish object in the toilet with a little blood on it. I called Athun right away.

"Athun here."

"Athun, something just came out of me! It's gross looking, like brownish with some blood."

"Just came out of you? Like when you were walking, you felt it?"

"No, when I went pee. It's in the toilet!"

"Did you flush it?" he asked.

"No, I called you right away."

"Okay, I'll come over when I'm finished with my patients for the day."

"When is that?"

"A couple of hours, probably..."

"Athun!"

"Cora, it's the best I can do."

"I'll just take a picture and send it to you."

"It's probably your mucus plug."

"Mucus what?"

"Google it! It means baby is coming soon. I can check you later on. Okay?"

"I'll just be at your place when you get home," I sighed.

"Okay, I'll see you soon."

"Bye," I said, hanging up a little annoyed Athun didn't seem at all concerned.

When Weston arrived home, I told him I was going to Athun's house, but would be back for dinner.

"Everything okay?" he asked.

"He's going to check me to see how my pregnancy is going."

"Check you...how?"

"He has these monitor things and he brings home the ultrasound machine from work, too."

"Seriously?"

"Yeah! He's helped me throughout my entire pregnancy."

"Isn't that a little weird?"

"It's super weird, but convenient...very convenient actually."

"All right."

"I'll see you soon," I said, giving him a kiss and leaving. When I got to Athun's, he still wasn't home. I took Moose for a walk around the neighborhood and started feeling this burning sensation in my lower back. I sat on the couch nodding off when Athun came through the door.

"Honey, I'm home," he said, putting his bag on the table. I smiled at him, amused. He looked so incredibly good looking in his hospital scrubs.

"Let me eat something. I'm starving and then I'll check you, okay?"

"Okay."

"You don't look very happy, Cora."

"I'm so uncomfortable! I think I'm ready for baby to be out."

Athun fixed us hot tuna melts. They were delicious!

"Okay, take your pants off. It will just make this much easier and lay down on the couch."

"Wait, what?"

"I'm going to check you."

"Check me how?"

"I'm wearing gloves! This isn't at all sexual!" he said in exacerbation.

"You're going to stick your fingers up my lady parts?"

Ugh!

"I have to see if you're progressing."

I haven't shaved!

"No, no, no, I can't. Don't you have some monitors or how about the ultrasound machine?"

"Nope, just these two fingers right here. Take them or leave them."

This is SO embarrassing.

"Athun, that is just too awkward for me!"

"I'm going to be the one delivering your baby, so you better get over it and soon!"

"Fine, just finger me..." I said, throwing my arms up in defeat.

"I'm not fingering you! This is NOT sexual!"

I placed my hands over my eyes. "Just do it!"

"Frog leg it for me."

"WHAT?" I cried, whipping my hands off my eyes and sitting up.

"Just put your knees up and let your legs fall to the side. You really are something else today!"

Oh...

I laid back down and closed my eyes again. Athun inserted his fingers into my vagina. I felt super awkward as he felt around.

This was ridiculous! *What would Weston think?*

"Oh yeah, you've begun the labor process, two centimeters," he said with a giant grin. He took his gloves off and went and disposed of them in the trash. I quickly stood up, pulling my underwear and pants back up.

"What does that mean?"

"You have to make it to ten centimeters before you're in full labor and can push, so eight more to go."

"So what do I do now?"

"Oh, you could stay two centimeters for a while. Some women go weeks without any change or you may go tomorrow."

"Go?"

"Into active labor. Didn't you read any of the pamphlets I gave you? You need to time your contractions. When they are every four to five minutes apart, just call me and we'll go to the hospital."

"This is crazy! I still have three weeks left until my due date."

"This stuff happens all the time. Don't worry, you'll be fine. Go home and take a bath. It may speed up the process if you relax."

"What if you're in another emergency c-section or you're tied up with a patient when I need to go to the hospital?"

"I'll make it happen! I'll be there." Athun could sense my frustration and gave me a hug. I took a deep breath in and exhaled.

"Thank you for invading my vagina tonight," I snickered, sarcastically.

"Hey, you're the one that didn't want to come to my office. I could've had one of my nurses check you."

"I know," I said, hugging him back. "I'm lucky to have you."

When I arrived back home to Weston, I told him and Olivia

to eat without me. I wasn't at all hungry. My lower back started hurting even more that night, so I decided to take Athun's advice and bathe. Two hours later, I lay there wondering when baby would be here. Olivia and Weston checked on me a few times, but I kindly kept reminding them that I was just needing some relaxation time.

I slowly got out of the bath and rubbed some pain reliever ointment onto my back. By the time I laid down next to sleeping Weston, the pain had subsided and I was able to get to sleep.

Not too long after I awoke to shooting pain grabbing at my lower abdomen and radiating through my lower back. After a minute or so, it went away. I took out my phone. It was ten o'clock. I lay there wide-awake, wondering how long I could tolerate this for. Five minutes later the pain was back again. I started watching the time on my phone, wondering if this is what contractions felt like.

An hour later and the pain had become every four minutes. I couldn't handle it anymore.

"Weston." I shook his shoulder. "Weston," I whispered again.

"What is it, Cora?"

"I'm in a lot of pain. I don't think I can take much more. Can you call Athun?"

I handed him my phone as tears started to escape my eyes. The pain was so severe. Weston got up and put some pajama pants on, leaving the room. He came back moments later telling me that Athun was on his way.

I propped myself up on all fours like a dog and shoved my face into my pillow. Weston rubbed my back. When the pain went away, I looked at Weston.

"I think it's hospital time."

"Did your water break?"

"No. Is it supposed to?"

"Yeah. I mean, that's when I took Raina to the hospital."

"Shit. What's happening to me then? I can't take it, Weston."

"Cora?" I heard Athun calling from the hallway. Weston left to get him.

"Athun, Weston. Weston, Athun," I groaned. I watched them shake hands.

"We've met once, at the bike trail," Athun said.

"Right. Athun, make this pain stop, please," I begged. Athun was by my side with his arm over my back.

"This better be active labor, Cora. I was busy entertaining a hot date when Weston called."

"With who?" I rolled over, sitting up and looked at Athun.

"I found her on some dating website."

"What?" I asked, grabbing Athun's hand and squeezing. I closed my eyes.

"Don't talk, just focus on the rise and fall of the contraction. It's going to go up, up, up and then come down, down, down," Athun said, softly.

I opened my eyes when the contraction was over. "You can't just go out with someone from the internet! She could be posing as a girl and really has a penis. It happens all the time! I just read an article about it."

Athun burst out laughing. "Lay down...I'll check you." I laid down onto my back. "I saw you all week and you don't even tell me you're going on a date? What the hell?"

"Do you want me to leave you two alone?" Weston asked, his tone laced with sarcasm.

"No," we replied in unison.

Athun began helping me pull my pants down.

"Woah, woah! What are you doing, dude? This is my

girlfriend."

"He's checking me," I said.

"This is not at all sexual. I'm seeing how far dilated she is."

"Weston, just turn around," I told him. Weston turned his back, mumbling something along the lines of 'not cool.' I turned my attention back to Athun.

"Does she have a job? Where does she live? Any children?"

"Impossible woman," Athun said like he always did. He was smiling big now. "You're seven centimeters, Cora. You're going to the hospital with me right now. Baby is coming tonight!"

"I'm not ready! I need more time!"

"Where's your hospital bag?" Weston asked.

"I don't have a hospital bag! Athun said I had three weeks left."

"Cora, I told you time and time again that baby comes when baby wants to. Didn't you read anything? There was a list of what you needed to pack."

"Just grab that bag right there and shove some underwear in it!" I said in frustration.

"No. The hospital will provide you with underwear," Athun said.

"Yeah, you'd ruin any underwear you brought, Cora," Weston chimed in. "The hospital underwear is much better."

"THAT'S IT!" I seethed through gritted teeth. "I am so sick of you two telling me what to do. This is my body! Neither of you even have vaginas!" I yelled. I grabbed my bag out of Weston's hand, shoved some clothes inside and waddled my way through the bathroom and into the hallway. I stopped, bending over and using the wall as support as I pushed through my next contraction.

Athun pushed on my lower back, which alleviated a lot of

the pain.

"Ugh, thank you," I whined when the contraction was over.

"We're just trying to help," he whispered in my ear.

"I know...sorry. Less talking and more moving, please."

Weston appeared, handing me my purse.

"I need to be there with you, but I have Olivia. I don't know what to do."

I handed him my phone. "Call my mom. Tell her I'm in labor and going to the hospital. She'll come stay here with Olivia. I know she will."

"Okay," he said, kissing me on the lips. He looked concerned.

"I'll be okay," I assured him.

"She'll be okay," Athun said, slapping him on the back, knocking Weston out of his daydream.

"I love you," Weston said.

"I love you, too. I'll be fine, Weston."

We made it out of the house and into Athun's BMW.

"We have to hurry! I don't want your water to break in my car."

"You jerk!"

I heard Athun snicker.

"Just think, a year ago I wasn't even a thought in your mind. Now here we are, you're driving me to the hospital to deliver my baby."

"You were always a thought in my mind," Athun said, as his cellphone went off. He grabbed it to read a text message.

"You can't text and drive! It's illegal! Give me that!" I demanded, taking his phone away.

"It's my date. I told her to stay at my house and I would be right back. I didn't honestly think we'd be going to the hospital right now. What'd she say?"

"She's getting tired and wants to know if she should stay there. No, she needs to leave! She doesn't even know you. What the hell is she thinking? Like, hello, go home! You two can catch up another day."

"Cora, do I sense some jealousy?"

"No!"

"Tell her I'm delivering a baby and I'm not sure when I'll be home."

"Fine." I text her back from Athun's phone, telling her he was delivering his best friend's baby. Maybe that would scare her off.

"Ugh, she says 'that's so cute.' Gross! I don't like her...I already know."

"Cora, you're being ridiculous! I wanted you, but you didn't want me. Remember?"

"Are we really having this conversation right now?" I asked, grabbing Athun's hand to squeeze through my next contraction. Athun started to talk.

"Don't talk," I growled through clenched teeth. When my contraction ended, I let go of Athun's hand.

"Sorry, I just need to concentrate through the pain. What do you want me to tell this girl?"

"Tell her to stay if she wants to and if not, to lock up when she leaves."

"Fine...done," I said. I clicked the screen off to his phone and then another text came though that read, "I'll stay," with a wink face. I was annoyed and I didn't even know why. I was relieved when we pulled into the hospital parking lot.

"Athun, I'm sorry I'm so nasty. I just want you to find a nice girl who doesn't see you're a doctor and use you for your money or cheat on you. I want her to like me. In high school, I hated when you would talk about this amazing new girl you found, only to meet her and she would turn her nose up at our friendship, like I was no good for you."

Athun put his SUV in park. "Can we not go there? That was high school. It was so long ago."

"Okay," I said, looking down at the floor mat.

"I love you, I really do," Athun said, grabbing my face and making me look at him.

"I love you, too," I said softly.

"Good. Now let's go have a baby!" he beamed, closing his door and running around to my side. He grabbed my bags and then looped his arm through mine. We walked to a door on the side of the hospital. Athun grabbed his badge out of his pocket, swiping it to open the door, then threw the lanyard and badge around his neck.

"Look at me, special treatment," I teased and Athun smirked.

"Can you walk? It's not far."

"I'm okay."

We made our way down a long hall and stopped at a set of elevators. Athun swiped his badge again and the elevator door opened. I read a large sign on the wall, FOR STAFF ONLY. He hit the button for the third floor. When the elevator stopped and the door opened, we were greeted by several nurses.

"Dr. Lom," I heard one say, looking surprised.

"Dr. Lom, I wasn't expecting to see you," another nurse said.

"Ladies, this is my best friend, Cora. I'll be delivering her baby here tonight. Molly, you want to take her to an open room and get her hooked up? I'll be in shortly."

Oh no, he's leaving me. Why?

"Are you able to walk?" the nurse asked.

"Yes," I replied.

"Okay, this way then." I stared at Athun, reluctant to follow the nurse.

"I'll be right there," he assured me. "I promise."

I turned and followed her. "My name is Molly and I'll be your nurse this evening. Is this your first?"

"Yes."

"Oh, how exciting. Okay, if you could head into the bathroom and take all your belongings off, then place them into that bag right there. I'll write your name on it and hang it on the back of the door. The hospital is not responsible for anything lost or stolen. There should be a johnny in front of the toilet. Put it on, opening goes in the front."

"My jewelry too?"

"Necklace off and anything else can stay."

"Okay," I said and shut the door.

I waited until my contraction passed to get dressed. I had just enough time to get my belongings into the bag the hospital had provided when another contraction came. They were heinous, the worst pain I had ever experienced.

When I opened the bathroom door, the nurse was waiting for me at the computer located next to the bed.

"Okay, come have a seat. I'm going to put two monitors on you, a blue one and a pink one. One is to measure your contractions and the other is to monitor your baby's heartbeat."

"Okay."

She placed the straps around my belly and moved them around until she got what she was looking for. I could hear the baby's heartbeat. Tears sprung to my eyes. The nurse saw my tears fall and smiled.

"Always a lovely sound to hear, isn't it?"

"It is."

Just then, Athun appeared.

"Can I have a moment please, Molly, with Doctor Lom?"

"Sure."

Athun looked puzzled. "What is it, Cora?"

"Athun, did you setup the adoption?"

"It's all set. When I deliver the baby, I won't put the baby to your chest. The nurses will examine the baby, make sure it is healthy and breathing and we'll take him or her right out of here. Okay?"

"Okay," I said starting to cry.

"It's okay. People give their baby up for adoption all the time. You're giving this baby a better life."

But am I?

Weston appeared in the doorway.

"Everything okay?" Weston asked when he found me crying alone with Athun.

"She's okay," Athun answered, excusing himself and returning with Molly.

Athun sat on a stool by the foot of the bed and Weston sat in a chair up by my head, holding my hand while the nurse fired off questions. I answered all of her questions about my past and present health. When it came time for questions pertaining to the baby's father, I took one look at Weston and lied, telling the nurse this baby was his. I started fumbling for answers about Weston's job occupation. I didn't even know the name of his company. I was relieved when Weston chimed in, answering her questions. I felt like a stupid woman.

I closed my eyes. I started to feel like I was a live performance, putting on a show. I was terrible at lying. They asked me if our home had heat and plumbing. *Why would the hospital need to know this if I was giving the baby up for adoption?* I was about to go mad just before the questions ended.

When another woman appeared pushing a cart and telling me she was there to do in-take paperwork and collect my health insurance information, Weston and Athun could sense my aggravation. I closed my eyes and worked through the contractions as I listened to them give her the information she needed.

Right after she left, a male nurse appeared and wanted to draw my blood. When the commotion was over, Molly checked me again. I was fully dilated now, but my water hadn't broken yet.

"We can wait to see if it will break on its own or I can break it for you," Athun said.

"Does it hurt?"

"Not at all. You will feel a warm rush of liquid and then shortly after you will feel a sudden urge to push."

"How will I know?"

"Oh, you'll know," Molly replied, smiling.

"Okay, I want this over with. Just do it!"

"Okay," Athun said. He put his gloves on and grabbed this long object from the table that was wrapped in plastic. I watched as he pulled the wrapping off. It looked like a long chopstick. "Ready?" he asked.

"Ugh...I guess."

"Okay, just lay there like you do, frog-legged. This won't hurt at all, I promise."

I closed my eyes and squeezed Weston's hand. I felt the object inside me and then a warm rush of liquid, just like Athun had said.

"Wow, that didn't hurt at all."

"Good. Molly, will you go get her the ball? We'll have her sit on that until she's ready."

"Sure," Molly answered, leaving and then coming back with a giant yoga ball.

"All right, I want you to sit on this at the edge of the bed. Here's a pillow if you want to lay your head down. You can sway side to side on it or some women do a light bounce."

Athun helped me out of bed and onto the ball. Liquid poured out of me onto the floor.

"Shoot Athun, it's getting all over the floor."

Athun smirked. "It's fine, Cora. That's perfectly normal. Just sit on the ball and relax."

Ah! How is he acting so nonchalant right now?

"Wait. Am I going to get some pain medicine?"

"You've made it this far and you're doing remarkable!"

Just then I heard a woman screaming from across the hall.

"Is that lady giving birth right now?"

"Yes," Molly replied.

"Did she have medicine?"

"Yes."

"Athun!"

"Cora, you were walking at seven centimeters. Trust me, you'll do fine!"

"You're doing wonderfully! You work really well with your body," Molly said. I was so scared. I knew this was the calm before the storm.

I felt another contraction coming. Athun moved behind me and massaged my lower back.

"This is called the counter-pressure point technique...you go right here...just like this. It will help her through the contraction," Athun told Weston.

"Okay," Weston said.

"I'm going to step out now. Molly will be in and out, too. Press the call button when you think it's time. Okay?"

"You're leaving?" I asked, whining.

Athun started chuckling. "I'll be just down the hall. I have to check e-mails, do things doctors do."

I sent him a venomous look. I knew he was lying to me. He was going to go call his date. I put my face into the pillow again, screwed my eyes shut in pain and waited for the contraction to end. They were getting longer and closer together now. I was exhausted and didn't have much fight left in me.

Weston worked on my back, massaging me like Athun had.

"Did I do it right?" he asked.

"Perfect, thanks."

This may be the most intimate moment I've ever shared with anyone. If you asked me who I'd share my most intimate moment with, I definitely would've never answered with the name Weston Ekelhart, but here we were and it didn't feel strange at all.

"I'm so fucking scared right now," Weston breathed.

I picked my head up and looked at him. "I'm about to have a bowling ball pass through my vagina! I'm beyond scared."

"I don't think I can do this. I thought I could, but I feel like I can hardly breathe. I mean, last time I was here like this, I lost my whole world."

"Weston, look at me," I said, softly.

He placed both his hands over his head. I had never seen him like this. He was sweating and growing more anxious by the second.

"Weston, stop! It's not going to happen again. It's not!"

"You don't know that!"

"I do. I spent so long being unhappy...years, Weston! Then, I left to come here and found you, someone who makes me so incredibly happy. The feelings I have for you and Olivia are ones I always dreamed of having, ones I never thought were truly possible. I'm not going anywhere. We can do this, I promise you!"

It was clear that what happened to Raina had left Weston

shattered in pieces. I grabbed his head and hugged him. "Stay with me, please."

It was so hard to see him like this. It was even harder trying to stay strong for him while I was in this ungodly pain.

"Okay," he breathed after a moment.

I felt an insane amount of pressure, like I had to go to the bathroom.

"Holy shit! Holy shit! I think it's happening! Oh no, oh no!" Weston pressed the call button and Molly was in the doorway, followed by Athun.

"She thinks it's time."

"Okay," Athun said. They all helped me back onto the bed. "Now lay back and put your knees up." I did just what Athun told me.

"Good. Now hold your legs back to your body. I'm going to have you push on your next contraction." The nurse looked at the screen. "Okay, there's one coming now," she said.

"Take a deep breath in Cora, hold it and push." I inhaled as much as I could and pushed with all my might.

"Woah, woah, hold it! I can see baby's head!"

I let out a breath and relaxed my legs.

"Get those legs back up to your chest. When you feel your next contraction, I want you to do the same thing, like you just did!"

I pushed again.

"Excellent. Do you want a mirror so you can see?"

"No!"

"Reach down and touch the baby's head!" Athun said. I could hear the excitement in his voice.

"Gross, no!"

I heard Athun chuckle. He wore a plastic protective shield over his face. I cringed, thinking how gross it was that stuff could fly out of my vagina and hit him in the face.

"Another coming, sweetheart," Molly said.

I pushed again.

"We're almost there. You just need to get the head out and I'll do the rest," Athun said. I was pushing with all my might. I just wanted it to be over with!

I felt another contraction and pushed. I let go, throwing my head back in exhaustion.

"I thought that was going to be it," Athun said. "You're almost there, give me everything you got!"

I was breathing heavy now. I felt another contraction coming and I waited just before the peak until I gave it everything I had.

"There it is, that's it! More...more. Push, Cora!"

I felt this excruciating pain quickly come and go and then the baby being pulled out of me.

"Baby is out," Weston said. "I can't believe it. You did great!" He stood up and bent over the bed, taking me into his arms and squeezing me tight. I felt the umbilical cord on my legs. Weston let go of me after the nurse asked if he wanted to cut the cord. I closed my eyes, not wanting to watch. I heard something about delivering the placenta...*placenta*? Then Weston mumbled he was feeling sick. When I opened them again, I saw Athun with his back to me, holding my baby...my flesh and blood. I heard a cry.

"Athun, let me see my baby."

"Cora, you shouldn't..."

"Athun, please!" I begged, reaching my arms out. He shook his head.

"We talked about this," he said. I felt the room grow silent as Molly stopped what she was doing and watched on. "It's only going to make it that much harder."

Athun was turned towards me now, but I still couldn't see my baby. My eyes locked with his as our standoff continued. I started to break down crying.

"Oh, did I forget to announce the sex?" Molly asked. "You have yourself a girl. Congratulations!"

I sat up and took one look at her. She was perfect. First I looked at her face, then her head and her ears. Athun didn't move a muscle as I pulled the hospital blanket back that he had wrapped her in. My eyes followed from her head down to her toes. She was every bit of incredible. I couldn't believe I had created this life that was before my eyes. I had this feeling inside my heart I had never felt before, this euphoric state of happiness. I was on cloud nine. It was like my whole world could fall apart this very instant and it didn't matter because I had my baby.

I shook my head at Athun.

"I can't do it. I can't give her away, Athun," I choked.

"Cora, it's what's right for the baby, not what's right for you."

I kept my eyes on her.

"I'll hide her. I'll keep her safe and he will never know. I want my baby!"

I could feel Molly and Weston continue to watch on.

"Don't give her your last name. She ought to take Weston's," he suggested, placing her to my chest. I stumbled to gauge his sincerity. *Is he mad?*

"Okay," I said, knowing Molly's head was now spinning with confusion.

"I'm going to clean up. I'll be in and out," Athun said, taking off his shield and gloves. He washed his hands and left the room. I can't believe he wasn't happy with my decision to keep my own baby. Maybe he was upset because he had wasted his time setting up the adoption. I looked at Weston, afraid he would be upset as well.

"Sorry, I couldn't do it. I really thought I could."

"We have nothing at home..."

"If you don't want to be with me anymore..."

"Stop," Weston said. "Nothing, not even a baby, is going to stop me from loving you. It's quite a surprise...I won't lie, but I see how you are with Olivia and I want you to experience your own. I'll make sure you have everything you need at home when we leave the hospital."

"Thank you," I said, crying. Weston was undeniably perfect.

"Can I get you anything?" Molly asked.

"No," I replied, peering down at my new baby girl.

"Could you show me where your coffee is?" Weston asked her.

"I can get you a cup. No problem," she replied.

"That's okay. I don't mind."

"Okay, follow me," she smiled.

"I'll be right back," Weston said, kissing me on the head.

Athun entered the room again.

"Are you mad at me for changing my mind?"

"No. I have a confession to make actually."

"What?"

"I never called the adoption agency."

"What? Why?"

"I know you better than you know yourself."

"So you just played along all this time?"

"I've always wanted children, to feel what you feel right now as you look at your baby. I want that as well. When you told me you were giving your baby up for adoption, I was quite surprised. I knew you wouldn't want to do it once you gave birth."

I grabbed his hand and squeezed it. Just then, Weston

appeared in the doorway. I took my hand back from Athun's, feeling like I had been caught with my hand in the cookie jar.

"I have to go. There's a beautiful woman sleeping in my bed! You will be fine and I'll be back tomorrow morning to check on you," Athun said, grabbing my face unexpectedly and giving me a sweet kiss on the lips.

"What was that for?" I asked, completely dumbfounded.

"You're amazing! You did absolutely beautifully! You are so strong, mentally and physically. I'm in awe of you."

"Thank you, from the bottom of my heart...for everything, Athun."

Athun got up from the bed. I watched him turn around just before he walked past Weston.

"What's her name, anyway?"

"I don't know. I haven't even thought about it."

"Well you think about it and goodbye for now."

"Bye, Athun," I said, smiling at him foolishly. Oh, did I love him dearly. *My best friend just delivered my baby. How many ladies can say that?*

Athun walked past Weston without a word. I wondered what they thought about one another.

"Hey Weston..."

"Cora," he interrupted me. "Does Athun know we're together?"

"The kiss? I have no clue what that was about. We're all exhausted, it's been a long night. What was Raina's middle name?"

"Rose. Raina Rose."

"I shall name her Lillian Rose then. Do you like it?"

"It's beautiful, but I have to tell you something."

"Oh no, it's too much. I won't do it then. I'll come up with a different name."

"No, it's perfect actually, because I lost Raina four years ago this very day."

"Really?"

"Yes, which is why I was literally on the verge of a mental breakdown while you just gave birth," Weston said, placing his hand over his chest like tonight's events had taken years off his life. "I have to apologize. I feel like I should've been doing more for you tonight or this morning...whatever time it is."

He grabbed the bridge of his nose, stifling a yawn. I, too, was exhausted.

"No. Please don't," I told him, reaching over and grabbing his free hand. "So that means today is Olivia's fourth birthday?"

"Her fourth birthday."

"Why didn't you tell me?"

"Truthfully, the day just snuck up on me. You were in the tub last night and I was worried sick about you and then you delivered in the wee hours of the morning. I blinked and the day was here."

"Wow. How does today feel, four years later?"

"I think this is a sign from Raina."

"I think so, too."

I called my parents to let them know they were officially grandparents.

"We're on our way," they cheered, which was the only thing they said other than hello and goodbye before hanging up. I put my phone down chuckling to myself.

"What?" Weston asked, watching me.

"My parents. They sound beyond excited to meet Lillian," I said, looking at her once more. "I can't tell you enough how happy I am that I decided to keep her. I can't believe I thought for one second I could give her away."

Right then the door opened and in walked a nurse I hadn't

met before. She introduced herself, letting us know she'd be our nurse until the next shift change this afternoon. We went over if Lillian had peed or pooped and if I had decided to feed her with formula or by breast.

Breast is best.

She then told me the next time I needed to feed Lillian and to call her if she wasn't latching. She was pleasant and nice. Everyone here was.

"Knock, knock," I heard my dad say as he entered the room with Olivia and my mother behind him. They had flowers and a basket my mother put on the table by the door.

"Some food for you if you get hungry. Hospitals never give enough food for mothers who just gave birth."

"Thanks, Mom." I told her. "Hi, Olivia."

Olivia handed me the flowers and Weston scooped her up into his arms. She instantly wrapped her arms around his neck and squeezed him tight.

"Happy birthday, Olivia," I heard him whisper in her ear. He closed his eyes and squeezed her back. I imagine this moment and even just saying those words to her were so emotional for him.

When she turned her attention back to me, I wished her a happy birthday as well.

"Weston! You didn't tell us it was her birthday today," my mother scolded him.

"It's...I'm sorry," he stuttered, shaking his head. "It's been a hectic last twenty-four hours. I don't even think she remembered it was her birthday today. I reminded her last week, but yeah," he said looking at Olivia again, "you're four today, Olivia. Four whole years."

I stuck my nose in the flowers and smelled them.

"Did you pick these out?" I asked Olivia.

"Yeah."

"They're beautiful and they smell so good!"

"Baby," she said, pointing to Lillian.

"This is Lillian. Come sit on the bed with me and you can hold her before her Grandma and Grandpa take her."

My parents moved closer to my bed to get a better look at their granddaughter. I glanced at all their faces, my heart completely filled by their response to Lillian. The feeling was new, like I had given all of them the most precious gift I could give. Even Olivia seemed to be in awe.

My mother and father took turns admiring Lillian. They stayed quite awhile and then when lunch was approaching, my mother told us she'd like to take Olivia out to lunch to a great kid friendly restaurant she had in mind.

"Would you like to come with us?" my mother asked Weston.

"I better go get some sleep. I think I'm starting to hallucinate," he laughed. "I just thought those were dog treats in that basket you brought."

"Oh gosh, no. Granola bars and trail mixes, but close," she chuckled. "You go and rest up."

"We remember what it was like," my father said.

I hugged Olivia close, holding her an extra minute. She had no idea how much I loved her. When my father came to my side to pick Olivia up, he rested his hand on mine.

"God has a plan for you, my brave daughter. I don't want you worrying. You just enjoy this moment and remember that. Okay?"

I wiped the tear that escaped my eye. He leaned down and kissed my forehead.

"He has a plan for all of you," he whispered.

CHAPTER FOURTEEN

I already had Lillian's nickname picked out. I would call her Lily. She didn't resemble Travis or me, but it was still too early to tell. Weston had left yesterday evening to be with Olivia on her birthday. I told Weston we would celebrate as a family when I was discharged tomorrow.

I called Weston right away.

"Morning, babe. How are you feeling today?" he asked.

"Weston, I never talked to Olivia about Lily. I mean, I had her feel my belly when she kicked, but we never actually had a discussion about what it all means. Now we're going to bring this little human home to live with us and Olivia has no idea. I'm really worried. I think you need to talk to her first."

"Okay, but that's your department. I wouldn't know what to say."

"Well, maybe we won't tell her it's her baby sister. I mean, we haven't been together that long and I don't want to rush things. We both rushed our relationship in our first marriage."

"What are you saying?"

"Nothing at all. What if we break up and I leave? It would crush Olivia to lose her sister."

"It would crush us both either way."

"Will you just tell her Cora is bringing Lily home tomorrow? I want her to be excited about it and not feel like the baby is taking me away from her. She's going to need time to adjust. Please?"

"Okay, I'll talk to her. I'll see you later on today, okay?"

"Okay. I love you, Weston Ekelhart."

"I love you too, Cora."

I'm sure Weston didn't dare say my last name. After all, it wasn't mine anymore.

I spent the rest of the day admiring Lily. She hardly opened her eyes. All she wanted to do was sleep, which was fine with me. I wondered if denying this moment from Travis was a sin that would have me sent straight to hell when I died. I was making a decision that I could never take back. I wondered if giving Lily Weston's last name would protect us from Travis. *Could he ever find out?*

I didn't like that my own daughter wouldn't share my last name, but there was nothing I could really do. I felt helpless. I needed to divorce Travis as soon as possible.

I heard a rattling of paper and I looked up to see someone shaking a bouquet of flowers in the doorway. I'd recognize that tattoo anywhere.

"Hi, Athun!"

"Hello, beautiful!" he said, stepping inside the room. "All alone?"

"No, Lily is with me."

"Lily. I love it."

"Lillian Rose. Lillian after my mother-in-law that just passed away and Rose from Weston's wife. Her name was Raina Rose."

"Wow, talk about a simple name packed with a hell of a lot

of meaning."

"I think so."

"How are you feeling?"

"Good. I've gotten up to go pee a few times and just walk around the room."

"Good. Let me just check your uterus."

"It's been checked."

"Okay, but I'd still like to see if it's going down in size. Are you cramping during breastfeeding?"

"Yes, but it's tolerable compared to giving birth." Athun let out a laugh, taking Lily from me and placing her in the hospital bassinet.

"You did extraordinarily well the other night. I mean it when I say I was in awe of you. No medicine and no screaming. You were as cool as a cucumber. I hardly ever see that. I feel so blessed to have been a part of it." Athun looked over, smiling at Lily. I saw a glisten in Athun's eyes.

I laid on the hospital bed for Athun to make sure my uterus was shrinking. This part was painful. "How was your date?" I asked, then sucked in a breath before enduring his torture.

"Didn't work out."

I let out a deep breath. *That wasn't so bad.*

"How come?"

"I get home and I'm tired, but I left her half naked in my bed, so I'm ready to get it on when I get home and all she wants to do is talk about the baby I just delivered."

"Oh, c'mon! That's really sweet."

"I thought so too, but oh no, it gets better. I tell her a little bit about you and how you're my best friend and well, now the lights are on. They were off when you called and we were about to...you know."

"Sex...I get it."

"Well, she asks me about the tattoo with your initials. I think oh, here we go again..."

"So what happened? She wasn't a fan?"

"She was mad! She actually yelled at me!" he said, pointing to his tattoo.

"Yelled? C'mon!"

"I swear! I mean, I just met the girl."

"Well, you did have her in your bed, so I think she thought she was a little more important than *some girl*."

"Who cares? Imagine me freaking out about some tattoo she had for her best friend? That's so weird!"

"I cock blocked you," I said, cracking up laughing.

"You owe me now. Lily is sleeping, maybe we could get a..."

"Athun!"

"I'm joking! You can't have any sex for six weeks, but that doesn't mean you can't..."

"Athun!"

"Okay, okay. I'm just kidding. In all seriousness, how is Weston with this whole being a dad to Lily thing? I mean, he looked a little freaked out when I left."

"He seems okay. I'm kind of sad Lily and I don't have the same last name though."

"So you gave Lily Weston's?"

"Yeah, to protect us."

"Well, it's what you have to do. Would you rather you give Lily Travis' last name and then he finds out you have a child and realizes it's his?"

"No. I need to divorce him. Now, more than ever I want a divorce. I need to fly out there, have him sign the paperwork and fly back the same day. I just want to be done with it."

"When?"

"As soon as I can. When's the earliest you think I'll be able to?"

"Woah, easy. Let's think about this. You're breastfeeding and Lily needs to eat every two hours."

"I know. I just want this Travis cloud to stop raining over my head. I want closure! I need to feel that Lily is safe!"

"I'll go with you. Can you hold off for a couple weeks? Let's get a surplus of breastmilk saved up. I mean, if you're only gone for a day you should be able to produce enough. Buy yourself an electric pump. I can show you how to use it. Oh, and some bottles."

I raised an eyebrow at him.

"Why do you get so annoyed when I try to help you?" he asked.

"I can figure out a breast pump. It's my breast."

"Fine, but I'm going with you. If he's back on heroin, who knows who is slumming around your house. He's met me…I'm just the best friend, so he doesn't have to know anything about Weston or Lily. Okay?"

"Okay. Two weeks. I'll find a lawyer to draw up the paperwork, then we'll fly out there and have Travis sign them. I'll give him everything so there's no argument. Then, we'll turn right around and come home." Athun held out his hand and I shook it.

"I'll come visit you at Weston's tomorrow since you are being discharged tomorrow morning. Is that okay?"

"Of course. I'll see you tomorrow."

Just as Athun was leaving, Weston walked through the door.

"Hi," I said, smiling.

"What were you two up to?"

"Oh, don't even. He's just my friend, I promise."

"Have you two ever slept together?"

"No. We've just kissed. He was checking my fundus."

"Your what? Let me guess, he had to insert his fingers into your..."

"No. Seriously, enough Weston. My fundus is right here," I said, pointing to my lower abdomen. "It's my uterus. He has to make sure it's slowly getting smaller. If not, it's a sign something isn't right. Okay?"

"Okay."

"So, did you talk to Olivia?"

"She's excited about being a big sister."

Ah! I told him no mention of big sister talk.

"You told her that?"

"Cora, I'm in love with you. I'm out of my mind in love with you. That's why I've been having such a tough time. These feelings completely took me by surprise. Here, I bought this for you a few weeks ago." He said, handing me a black velvet box.

Oh no.

"What is it?" I asked.

I already think I know...

"Open it," he urged.

I opened the box to find a ring. It had one big diamond in the middle and two small ones on either side.

"An engagement ring, for when you're ready."

"You mean, you're not going to propose?" I laughed.

"You're still married and I have to respect that. No rush, right? Here," he said, taking off his wedding ring and placing it in the box. Then he closed it. "I was thinking maybe you could ask me when you're ready."

I sat there, just staring at the box.

"You don't like my idea?" he asked.

"No, I love your idea! I thought I would have to beg you to take your wedding band off. I'm just surprised, that's all. I fell for you very early on, but you...it's like I have to push and pull and tug your love for me out of you."

"Well the truth is, I began talking to Raina when you started spending your nights at Athun's house. I was having so much guilt feeling the way I did about you. I knew you liked me and of course I wanted you...the entire time, but I couldn't make the move. It was like the death of Raina paralyzed me. I knew if I didn't act fast, I was going to lose you and I think that's why I eventually slept with you that night. I wanted to show you I did care about you. Sometimes I even found myself crying, asking Raina to give me some sort of sign. I felt like I needed her acceptance of you to be my wife and Olivia's stepmother."

Weston sat down in the chair next to my bed and placed his head between his legs. It was in this very moment, I could literally feel how real the struggle was that existed inside Weston's heart.

"And now you have your sign..." I whispered. Weston looked over at our sleeping Lily.

"She was born almost three weeks early. There's a one in three-hundred and sixty-five-day chance she was born on the same day Raina died and Olivia was born. It's Raina. She's telling me you're the one."

I couldn't help but cry tears of joy. I was so mad at Weston at the time because he couldn't give me the more that I wanted. It was so sweet hearing his confession.

"I need to talk to you about something," I said, wiping the tears from my cheeks.

"What is it?" Weston asked, moving next to me on the bed.

"I need to divorce Travis. I talked to Athun and he wants to come with me...to protect me, sort of speak. We'll be gone one day. I'll fly out in the morning and be back by night. Athun said I could pump milk for Lily and you could give her bottles..."

"I don't know. I don't like anything about it. I'd rather go with you than Athun."

"No! No way! Travis has already met Athun and knows he's just a friend. Travis might freak if he sees you and finds out we're together. I don't want to piss him off. I just need him to sign divorce papers."

"I mean, I guess I took care of Olivia all by myself. Surely I can take care of Lily for one day."

"Really? My mom and dad can help if you need anything. Thank you, thank you!" I said, wrapping my arms around his neck. "Trust me, I don't want to be away from Lily more than a minute, but I've had this divorce from Travis weighing on my mind for months. Now I'm so afraid he'll come looking for me and somehow find out about Lily. It's my worst nightmare."

"Okay. Just tell me when and I'll be there for you."

"You're incredible. Athun told me to give it a couple weeks to let my body rest and settle down with Lily. Besides, I need time to draw up the divorce paperwork."

"I agree. You just gave birth, Cora. As superwoman as you are, you need to rest."

"I promised Travis I would bring his truck back, but I don't want to drive it halfway across the country. What should I do? He really loves that truck. I think he'll be upset if I don't follow through on my word."

"I'll take care of it. He can have the camper too. Give him whatever he wants, Cora. Just be done with it."

"That's the plan," I said, leaning in and giving him a kiss. *Oh, I love this man!* I sat there looking at him, still unable to believe we just talked about marriage. He had on dark denim jeans, a black cotton crew neck t-shirt and he looked so incredibly desirable. It will be all I can do to wait these six weeks. *Weston*

Ekelhart. My dreamy grade school crush. My Weston.

****

I was all ready with Lily dressed in her going home outfit and my bag packed when Weston arrived at the hospital for our discharge. I had taken the two rings and put them on my necklace, which I now wore around my neck. The truth was, I was ready to take Weston's last name today, but I knew deep down I had to settle my unfinished business. I wasn't just in love with the thought of having the family I have always wanted, I was in love with Weston having my trust. I felt this sense of safety with him that I had never experienced before. Weston held the capability to turn my world upset down, but he never would. He was successful in every aspect of his life, which made him extraordinary.

"Earth to Cora. Are you ready?" Weston asked.

"Sorry."

"Everything okay? I know I gave you a great deal to think about last night..."

"I'm just so excited to start this new chapter of my life. I was deathly afraid to leave Massachusetts and now I'm dreading having to go back. I saw myself living in that camper and moving around from parking lot to campground, just trying to find my place in this world. It's hard to believe I found it right away. You gave me my life back."

"Believe me, it is you who gave me mine," he said, taking Lily who was strapped in her car seat and kissing me on my forehead. I followed him out of the room. The nurse cut the ankle bracelet from Lily's leg and offered me a wheelchair. I didn't want it, but of course Weston insisted I take it.

Ahhh, free to leave.

I felt good. I definitely didn't feel like I just gave birth. It felt like I just hiked a mountain because my legs were sore and overall, I was still a little fatigued.

I sat in the back and admired Lily the entire ride home. This was what love at first sight meant. I always thought that was the biggest myth I had ever heard, but now I have learned it's the truth. Lily is my love at first sight.

"My girls okay back there?"

My girls.

"Oh yeah. Where's our other girl?"

"Still with your parents. She absolutely adores them. I think the feeling is mutual actually."

"I'm sure it is. I bet she had both of them wrapped around her pretty little finger."

When we pulled into the driveway, there were a bunch of vehicles and a group of people.

No!

"Weston. Stop! Turn around."

"What is it?" Weston asked, as he continued down the driveway until I recognized their faces. *Phew*! I started to cry. Weston turned around and saw me crying. "Are you okay?"

"Yes. I feel like such an idiot. I thought your siblings were people coming to take Lily from me."

"Cora, look at me," Weston said, placing the truck in park and turning around. "I promise you that I will never let Travis or anyone take Lily from you. Get that thought out of your mind. I will always keep you, Lily and Olivia safe." He unbuckled his seatbelt and leaned over the middle seat, wiping the tears from my eyes. "Now I have a little surprise for you. Come."

Weston's siblings were at my door when I stepped out.

"Surprise," they said. Maura could hardly contain her excitement, bouncing towards me and wrapping her arms around me. She squeezed me so tight I lost my balance.

"Sorry," she laughed. I hugged her with equal strength. It was at this very instant I realized how much I had missed her! She looked stunning. All his siblings did. I hugged all six of them. It felt like a family reunion.

"What has it been, sixteen years?" I asked.

"That's what we were all thinking. You look great for just giving birth," Laura said. She was the second to oldest.

"Y'all have kids of your own now?" I asked.

"Weston didn't tell you? There are twenty cousins all together. Maura over here is the only one who isn't contributing."

"I'm going backwards in that department, actually," Maura laughed. "I just broke up with my fiancé of three years. Once a cheater always a cheater."

"Ouch. I'm so sorry!"

"Thanks. It's not me I want to talk about, though. You and my brother?" Maura asked, right as Weston retrieved Lily from the car.

"You never would've guessed, huh?" he asked her and all his siblings shook their heads. We made our way inside. The house was spotless.

"Who cleaned?" I asked.

"We all did," Denise said. "Do you want to see the baby's room?"

I looked at Weston and made the I'm about to cry face. It had been years since someone had invested their time to work on something that would make me feel special. I felt overwhelmed. I climbed the stairs and walked down the hallway, stopping at Olivia's room.

"Who did this?" I asked, looking around at the rainbow painted walls. Everything was transformed into the Trolls theme. She had a trolls bed set, lamp, laundry basket and waste basket.

"We all helped with Olivia's room and Lily's," Maura said.

"Has Olivia seen this yet?"

"No, we were waiting for you first."

"Wow, thank you."

"Don't thank us yet. Come see this other room!"

I walked down the hall, past the bathroom and stopped at the other guest bedroom that was now Lily's room. I was completely blown away. There was a rocking chair filled with wrapped gifts and bags spewing onto the rug. There was a crib, a changing table, diaper pail and swing. Everything was different shades of pink and white. From the window treatments to the crib sheets to the beautiful lamp, it was all spectacular! There were even balloons tied to the rocking chair that read "It's a Girl" and "Congratulations."

"Guys, this is too much," I gushed, bringing them all in for a group hug. "Thank you."

"It was nothing," Maura said.

"We had so much fun decorating the rooms," Lesley added.

Just then, Lily started to fuss. I turned to see Weston with her. It was the perfect sight to see.

"I think Miss Lily is ready for her feeding," Weston announced.

I checked the time on my phone. Like clockwork, it was just past the two hours from her last feeding. "I'll go feed her in our bedroom. If you'll excuse me for a few minutes, everyone," I said, taking Lily from Weston and heading back downstairs to our bedroom.

Wow. So this is what being a part of the Ekelhart family feels like. Twenty cousins? That's amazing! I was never close to my cousins, but I would certainly love it if Olivia and Lily were. There must be cousins of all ages. I think there was a ten-year gap from the oldest Ekelhart kid to the youngest.

Just then I heard the door open and saw Maura stepping in. I figured I would feel shy breastfeeding in front of others, but I didn't feel that way at all. Maura and I used to shower together all the time when we were kids.

"Hey. I hope you don't mind. I just don't know when the next time will be that I'll be able to catch you alone."

"No problem. You look so different, Maura. I hardly recognized you! You're so...glamorous."

"That's what Hollywood will do to you."

"Wow. Weston says you're in the fashion industry."

"I love it. I just dressed Reese Witherspoon for the Oscars."

"No way! I'm so jealous. She's my favorite actress."

"So you and my brother?" she questioned. I felt my cheeks heat with embarrassment.

"I know. So weird, right? If I stop and think about it, it's still hard for me to believe."

"Have you two slept together?"

"Oh my gosh! Maura! I'm not telling you that...he's your brother."

"Stepbrother. He says you're still married."

"I am. You remember Paul Bennett? We went to high school with him. It's his older cousin, Travis Cavanaugh. I left with him the same week I met him. It was like I drank some love potion and I was under his spell. He played the guitar and he promised me he was going to make it big..."

"In Massachusetts?"

"I know. I was such an idiot! I wish my parents never let me go. I mean, after Travis worked odds and end gigs, he realized he wasn't going to get some major record deal so he opened a landscaping company. He was successful for a while and then he started doing drugs."

"Let me guess, marijuana? Isn't that when we stopped hanging out...you were allergic or something and couldn't be around it."

"No, I didn't like the people who were smoking it with you. Besides, it really did make my eyes itchy. I only wish Travis smoked pot instead of heroin."

"Holy shit!"

"I know."

"I'm so sorry. So, do you think you still love him?"

Oh, Maura! Still so inquisitive.

"Of course I do! I mean, you don't stop loving someone just because drugs have a hold on them. He's a completely different person sober."

"I can't believe your parents let you go..."

"I couldn't wait to get the hell out of here. I was so suffocated. I hadn't ever been on a plane and I had always wanted to see the East Coast. My parents weren't fond of the idea. They made me promise I'd go to college."

"And did you?"

"Oh yeah. I enrolled as soon as I stepped foot in Mass." I smiled to myself, thinking I had my life together because I was going to college and now looking back, realizing how reckless I was. "I married Travis less than ninety days after I met him. It was just the two of us on the beach. I have no idea why he even asked me, but I thought I would have my fairytale ending."

"Don't we all."

"So what's your guy story? He cheated?"

I thought Weston mentioned Maura was married...

"Oh yeah, caught him red-handed. He accidentally butt dialed me while he was cheating on me. Three years I gave that asshole..."

"That's horrible."

"Am I interrupting?" Athun asked, with his body halfway inside the room. "Weston told me I could find you in here."

"Maura, do you remember Athun Lom? He graduated with us. Athun, this is Maura Ekelhart."

They nodded their heads at one another and shook hands.

"You two were inseparable in high school," Maura said.

"Oh yeah. Athun was my beer pong partner in high school. Now he's busy delivering my baby."

"You're a doctor?" Maura perked up.

"Yes. In my fourth year now."

"Wow. That's so hot!"

"Yeah? What do you think about this tattoo? I got it in high school for Cora," Athun asked, lifting his arm for Maura to see. I started cracking up laughing. *Was he serious right now?*

"That is the sweetest thing I have ever seen. Did you know he did this for you, Cora?"

"Oh yeah, he showed me that same day."

"Most girls hate it," Athun said. "They're all jealous of those two initials right here."

"Really? I think it's really cute."

"Awesome. Are you available?" Athun asked Maura.

"Yes, but I'm heading back to California tomorrow."

"Bummer. I was going to ask you to dinner tonight."

"Well, that doesn't mean I can't go to dinner."

"Okay, enough you two," I said. Weston appeared in the doorway.

"Your parents are here. Olivia is ready to see her new little sister."

I finished feeding Lily and left Athun and Maura giggling in the bedroom. "Go get your sister. Athun is hitting on her right now," I whispered as I brushed by Weston.

"Better than him hitting on you," he said, smirking.

True.

"Cora!" Olivia shouted when she saw me. I bent down as Olivia ran towards me.

"Hello, sweet girl. Would you like to see Lily again?"

I held Olivia in one arm and Lily in the other, glancing up at my parents and smiling.

"Oh, I can't wait to get my hands on her," my mother said.

"She's just the tiniest thing I've ever seen." My father said to my mother. All I was watching was Olivia admiring Lily. I had no relation to Olivia and Olivia had no relation to Lily, but it sure felt like I was holding my two daughters. I swallowed down my emotions as Olivia went about touching Lily's hair, her nose and finally landing on her hand.

"Can I hold her?" Olivia asked.

"Sure," I replied, turning and realizing everyone had been watching us. Weston had tears in his eyes. I smiled at him. Yet another one of my purest moments. Olivia climbed up onto the couch and I placed Lily in her arms. Denise called Weston over and took our picture, then a few snapshots of the proud big sister with her new baby.

When Olivia was finished admiring her little sister, we all headed upstairs to open gifts.

"Where did all of these come from anyway?" I asked.

"Well most of them are from us," Weston replied, "but your parents brought some from people who attend his church."

"Oh yeah, when you're ready, hopefully the congregation can meet my granddaughter," my father said, smiling from ear to ear.

I couldn't believe the amount of generosity. I was literally overwhelmed by the end. I had anything and everything I could ever dream of for Lily.

After the gifts, Weston and his siblings cooked dinner for everyone and my parents took turns holding Lily. I was really falling in love with my new life. I couldn't think of one puzzle piece that was missing.

"Dinner is ready," Denise announced. We all headed to the dining room.

Every time I looked up from the table, I saw something new to admire. Olivia's hair had grown a little longer, Maura still had the scar on her temple from when Weston accidentally shot her with his BB gun and then there Athun was, laughing about something with my parents. I was on cloud nine and never coming down.

As the night went on, everyone said their goodbyes and Olivia was tucked into bed. Athun and Maura were the last ones to leave so I invited them to stay. I wanted to show Maura the VHS tapes from our childhood.

"Actually we're going out," Maura said, giggling and glancing at Athun. "Not to mention, you need to get off your feet and get some rest. We can look at the tapes another time. Soon!"

"Yeah. It's time we catch up from high school," Athun chimed in.

Catch up? They never even talked in high school!

"Oh, I didn't know you two knew each other from school. Well, enjoy yourselves," I said.

Athun never made eye contact with me. He probably knew I'd disapprove of a one-night stand with my childhood best friend. *Ugh, why did I even care?* It was none of my business and I genuinely wanted to see him happy.

I finally realized how exhausted I was when they left.

"I love Lily's bedroom, Weston, but would you mind if she slept in our room for a little while?"

"Not at all. I did the same with Olivia. She was up every

few hours."

"Who watched her during the day?"

"I did. I'd go to work and get the guys started. I'd just place Olivia in her car seat and she was content with that for a little while."

"Wow. I can't even imagine trying to run a company with a newborn."

"You just do what you have to do."

I left Lily with Weston to go find the co-sleeper I had received earlier. I placed it in between us and put Lily in it. She was such a good baby. All she wanted to do was sleep.

"Don't get used to this. She's sleeping great for us now, but in a couple of weeks we'll have to actually work at getting her to sleep."

"Really?"

"Well, I guess I can't really say for sure, but that's how it was with Olivia."

"It's weird to be learning about babies from you. I do know a lot about them, but definitely not newborns."

"It's hard. I think I was awful at it and as soon as one stage ends, another one starts. It's like I never knew what the hell I was doing because when I finally figured it out, Olivia would start something new."

"I'm sure you'll be a great help. Olivia also," I said.

"I'm here for you. Anything you need, just ask me."

"Thanks," I said, leaning over Lily and giving Weston a kiss.

"I have to tell you something, Cora, but I hope you're not upset with me…"

"What? What is it?" I asked, afraid of what Weston was about to say.

"Lenny decided to do the treatment. Ben called me while I was here at home and you were in the hospital. He wanted me to let you know."

"Oh my gosh."

"I told Ben you had just given birth to a baby girl and were still in the hospital, but that I'd let you know when you were discharged."

"Thank you."

"Are you mad? I knew you'd want to know right away so I planned on telling you that day and then I got to the hospital and you were being discharged. Then my family came..."

"Mad? Why would I be mad? That's amazing news! I wonder what changed his mind. Ben said he could live years with treatment. Wow. "I know how fond of him you've become."

"Can you arrange for us to go there and he can meet Lily?"

"Sure, but maybe when Lily is a little older? Or we can bring Lenny here for a visit," Weston said. "Those places are littered with germs. Lily's just a few days old."

"His own words are the reason Lily is sleeping between us right now. I'll never forget them. It's funny really, I wanted to help Lenny and help Olivia grasp the concept of money and I don't think I did either of those, but he sure as hell made all the difference in my life."

CHAPTER FIFTEEN

Weston stayed home with me for the first week, which was a lot of help. I never knew how much work a newborn was. For starters, I was completely beat from lack of sleep. Lily would wake me up every two hours on the dot, which meant three times during the night. Weston slept right through any noise Lily and I made.

Then, during the day I would feed Lily. In between her feedings I would try to feed myself. I swear I was hungrier than when I was pregnant. I'd try to fit in a shower for me, a bath for Lily...diaper changes...oh the diaper changes. What was the point of having a diaper if Lily pooped right through them? I think she marked me, Weston and Olivia in the first week. Poor Olivia was afraid to hold her again. If I had any spare time, it was spent trying to nap while Weston and Olivia looked after Lillian. I cannot fathom those who had triplets or even twins for that matter!

After the first week, Weston would come home around noon to help with Lily and then make dinner for us. He was my dream come true...the red cherry on top of my rainbow sprinkled twist. I prayed he always stayed this way. Time and time again I thought back to my marriage with Travis and all the pain I had endured over the years. I deserved Weston. I truly felt like he was my light at the end of that very dark tunnel I once crawled through.

****

Athun called the night before we were due to leave for Massachusetts.

"Hey, we still on?" he asked.

"You bet! Thank you. Just knowing you're coming with me is making it that much more tolerable."

"I'd do anything for you, Cora."

"I know. You are the best friend anyone could ever ask for."

"I'll pick you up at five tomorrow morning. Okay?"

"Perfect! See you then."

I had my breast pump as my carry-on, which I had thrown over my shoulder as I waited for Athun at the door. I was so nervous now. My heart was beating faster with every passing minute and I could feel my legs start to shake. *I'm okay. I'm okay. I'm okay*. I lied to myself. I was so afraid to see Travis again. *What if he was thin as bone, with his eyes sunken in again? Would I want to stay and help him? No! I couldn't! I wouldn't!*

"Morning. You ready?"

"No. I'm freaking out right now. I don't want to go anymore," I said, as Athun opened his door and ran around his SUV to open the passenger side door for me.

"I promise you will feel much better when all is said and done. Nothing is going to happen to you. He's going to sign the papers and we'll be on our way."

"But what if he doesn't? What if he turns into a rage? If he's high...who knows what he'll do. This is a bad idea..."

"Cora! Stop. I'll beat the shit out of him if he gets within a foot of you." Athun took my breast pump and placed it inside his SUV. I reluctantly got into his vehicle. I had this pit in my stomach that something wasn't right. I felt like I was going to be sick because I knew deep down when I felt this way, my intuition was usually spot on.

"Let's not think about it anymore," he said, closing my door and getting back in the driver's side.

"Let's talk about how hot Maura is and how she needs to move back here."

"Jeez. I completely forgot to ask you how things went. I've been so caught up with diapers and milking myself like a cow."

Athun chuckled.

"We went to a bar. Well, it was a restaurant, but we sat at the bar. There was a band playing and Maura wanted to be front and center."

"So you didn't play catch up?"

"Oh please. I never talked to the girl in high school. There was no catching up."

"You are such a horn dog! You probably just said anything to get what you wanted."

"No...not at all. I keep things real. I mean, I poured my heart out to you and was completely rejected. What does Weston have that I don't, anyway?"

"Can we not do this? I haven't even had coffee yet."

"No, really. Does he even have facial hair? He still looks like a kid...definitely not a man."

"He has the picture-perfect face for a poster of an all-American man," I said. Athun roared with laughter.

"What, because I'm half Mexican? I'm not all American..."

"You can be a real ass sometimes. You know that?"

"Sorry. I just don't get it. You said you found me

attractive."

"You are. You're super sexy and your body..."

"What's the problem then? Break it down for me."

"You and I never got there, Athun.."

"I don't get it."

"I fell in love with Weston first. And I'll admit in the beginning it was just the idea of him. Growing up all the girls wanted him and there was that curiosity factor. Like, what was it like?"

"To have sex with him?"

"No," I said, reaching my hand across the vehicle and playfully hitting him. "I'm being serious here."

"Me too."

"Oh."

"So what did you mean then?"

"I meant...what was it like to be wanted in return? To be loved by him. As far back as I can remember, Weston never took anything serious including relationships. He always had his arm draped over this girl one day and kissing the cheek of another one the next. But one girl? I never saw it. I just thought maybe I could be that *one* girl.

"And then you met Olivia..."

I smiled to myself.

"The moment I saw her, I wanted to know Weston's life. Then the more I learned, the less I got my hopes up. He wasn't the bubbly flirtatious kid I remembered."

"And yet you still fell in love with him."

"I know. Weird, isn't it? Falling for the same guy, yet a completely different one."

I glanced over at Athun who smiled back at me.

"Now back to Maura. She's over the top super model, huh?"

"Is she ever!" he said, slamming his hands down onto his steering wheel with enthusiasm and making me jump.

"Wow, I guess she made quite the impression."

"You think? Look at these claw marks on my back," he said, leaning forward as he drove and picking up the back of his shirt.

"I'd rather not. What the hell happened?"

"These aren't bad scratch marks, pure ecstasy actually. I think if anything, this tattoo turned her on! She's an animal!"

"So you took her back to your place?"

"We didn't make it. We had sex right where you're sitting."

"Oh, Lord," I said, placing my hand up over my face.

"What? We had sex in the backseat, too. She gave me the best blow job I've ever had."

"Okay, enough of that, thank you very much."

"What? If you're going to take your title back as my best friend, then you need to listen to my story about the best night of my life."

"I already have the title of your best friend," I said, thinking about how jealous I was of Athun and the ultimate one night stand he had with Maura. I wanted an amazing sex life. I couldn't wait for another month to pass, so I could have something called a sex life because right now, I don't think I could even say Weston and I had that. "What happened to wanting a wife and family?" I asked.

"I still want that. I'm not going to wait around for it, though. I mean, Maura had a flight scheduled to leave the next day. Wouldn't you bang the shit out of her? Look at the girl. She's not marriage material."

"True. She definitely belongs in Hollywood. Her home roots have long dried up."

When we parked at the airport, my nerves were creeping up again. We made it through the security check point without any problems and onto the plane just fine.

"Want a drink?" Dr. Lom asked, who insisted we fly first class. I wondered how much money he had.

"I'm breastfeeding!"

"Pump and dump."

"Huh?"

"Pump your milk when we get off the plane and then dump it out. You'll be fine."

"I could use a drink..."

Halfway through our flight and Athun had me plastered. I could barely walk to the bathroom. Athun had to practically carry me. He slipped into the bathroom with me.

"What are you doing?"

"C'mon Cora, mile high club!"

"Get out!" I said, pushing him out through the door and laughing hysterically. Athun was far too immature to be a doctor. I sat on the toilet chastising myself. *Why did I let myself get this drunk*? I prayed to the Lord above not to let me throw up. The last thing I needed was to show up to see Travis and puke at his feet.

When I stepped outside, I found Athun flirting with the flight attendant.

"Seriously, you're trying to get it on with the workers?" I asked, after she excused herself.

"No. She told me you were cut off," he replied, laughing.

"Too late. I cut myself off. How could you let me get drunk?"

"Oh, please. You were so wound up! We're going to get off this plane, drive to your house and demand this divorce! You're going to say, 'listen to me you son of a bitch, you owe me!'"

"I would never call Travis a son of a bitch. I hardly swear."

"You're too nice. If you didn't think about how everyone else was feeling you'd be having no problem right now."

True.

Athun paid an Uber driver to take us to my house. I was squeezing Athun's hand, with my head pressed against the seat in front of me. I closed my eyes.

"She's okay. She's getting married today, so she's just a little nervous," Athun explained to our driver.

"Oh...well...congratulations," the driver said.

"Can I pay you to stay here? This should only take five minutes. You name your price."

"Twenty dollars..."

"You sold yourself too short. I would've given you thirty!" Athun said, climbing out of the car and tugging me with him.

"You are something else, you know that? Getting married today? Try divorce, if I'm lucky," I scoffed.

"It's all I could think of. You're getting your divorce today! No ifs, ands or buts," he said, as we sat outside the front door. *I can't believe I just knocked on my OWN door*! I looked around and saw the grass hadn't been cut in a while. *Geesh, that was supposed to be Travis' specialty!* I noticed there were no vehicles in the driveway.

"Are you looking for Travis?" an older man asked.

"Yes. Have you seen him?"

"You just missed all the commotion. He was taken by ambulance about twenty minutes ago."

"Shit!" I said, jumping up off the front step. His words were sobering.

"You're his wife, aren't you? I think I drive your car."

"I'll be back to talk to you about that. No worries...you can have it. I just need to sign the title over to you," I hollered, as I jumped back into the uber car. "Hospital, right away!" I said to the driver.

"Which one?"

I rolled down my window.

"Do you know which hospital?"

"No. Try our closest one...Mercy."

"Mercy Hospital and please hurry," I said to the driver. I waved to my neighbor, noticing my car in his driveway on the way by his house. *Travis really gave my car away. I loved that car.*

When we arrived at the hospital, I ran inside as Athun paid the Uber tab. I stopped at the information desk. "Travis Cavanaugh. I'm his wife, Cora. Cora Cavanaugh. He was taken in by ambulance, maybe a half hour ago."

"Okay, ma'am. Just stay calm. We'll see where he is."

"Anything?" Athun asked, his warm hand on mine.

"No. She's looking to see if he's here." I looked at Athun, thankful he was here. It was then I saw a woman sitting in a chair all alone. She had her face in her hands and I could hear her crying. I walked towards her slowly.

"Ma'am..." I heard from behind me, but I didn't respond.

"Lillian? Lillian?" I called. The woman lifted her head and my eyes were met by my mother-in-law's.

"Cora..." she said, standing up and quickly walking towards me. Tears streamed down her face. "It's Travis. He overdosed. He's gone."

CHAPTER SIXTEEN

I watch Lillian as she admires her granddaughter.

"You are half of him," she tells Lily, who finds her grandmother's moving lips quite amusing. Lillian hasn't said Travis' name since the day he passed, but she sure tells Lily every day that she is half of him.

He was once my other half too...

I'm angry and I'm sad, but neither of those emotions are worth feeling when the person who caused them is no longer here. I've decided to swallow all the pain and let Lillian believe I named my daughter after her because of the love I have for her and not because I believed she had taken her last breath.

My ringtone from my phone made me jump. Athun.

"Hello?"

"What are you doing tonight?"

I laughed into my phone, wondering what Athun had up his sleeve.

"If you're asking if I can come out and play, must I remind you I am a milk machine. I swear Lily is going through a growth spirt."

"Meet me for dinner. Maura and I have some news."

"Maura? My Maura?"

"She's in town."

"You better not be moving to California."

"Just meet me for dinner and you'll find out."

I shook my head wondering how much more my heart could handle.

****

"You ready?" Weston asked, as I took his outstretched hand.

"You two enjoy yourselves. I know we will," Lillian says, as she holds Lily in one arm and wraps her other around Olivia.

"We'll be back shortly," I said, nervous to leave Lily for the first time.

"Nonsense! Take your time."

"Is everything okay?" Weston asked when we got into the truck. "You don't seem your bubbly self lately."

"Things are good," I sigh, swallowing down the tears that threatened to surface.

"If Lillian being here is too much..."

"No. She's a great help! I love having her here."

"Is it Travis? I know you still..."

I cut Weston off before he could even say the L word. *How could I love and loathe someone at the same time?*

"For the first time in my life, Weston, I feel like I can finally breathe. Like a weight has been lifted off my shoulders and someone had to die to make me feel that way. Do you know how horrible that makes me feel inside? I just want to run around the house yelling I'm free...I'M FREE! I can't, though and I won't because his mother, whom I love dearly, is holding our child."

Weston snaked his arm around me and pulled me in close

to his chest.

"I love you so much," I cried.

Happy tears.

"I love you too, Cora."

After a moment I sat back in my chair, wiping my eyes.

"So much for putting on all this makeup so I could look pretty for you tonight. I'm a red blotchy mess..."

"We don't have to meet Athun for dinner. I can order takeout and we'll eat in the truck."

"No. I want to hear Athun's news, but I'm not that hungry..."

"Well, what did you have in mind then?" he asked.

"Let's go to the jewelry store."

"The jewelry store?" he asked with his eyebrows raised.

"Yes. There's this man I want to marry, so I must buy him a ring."

"Athun?" Weston snickered.

"Very funny! I'm being serious, Weston. I want to marry you. I know I have your ring and mine, but I'll put them in a tiny box and who knows...maybe the kids will want them when they get older. I want a fresh start. Life is so incredibly precious. You know that and we still have so many years to live. I want to live them all with you."

A smile played across Weston's face. He wasn't just smiling though, he was gleaming. This look was one I had never seen before.

"Okay. First, the restaurant since we don't want to be late and then a ring for the lucky man in your life."

****

"Ekelhart, party of eight," Weston told the hostess.

"Right away. Follow me."

I didn't have time to question Weston before I was following him and the hostess to our table.

Eight?

Then there he was, seated at the furthest end of the table. Lenny. Next to him was Sherri. Tears formed instantly and I found myself drawn to the space between them.

"Sherri," I said, leaning down to hug her. "And Lenny! It's so nice to see you both."

"My son planned a special night," Sherri told me.

"He sure did. I'm a lucky girl."

"How are you feeling?" I asked Lenny while bending down and wrapping my arms around his neck.

"The doctors say I need this treatment, but they don't know what a tough bastard I am," he said. He smiled at Sherri. "Sorry, dear." Sherri seemed oblivious to Lenny's foul language.

"I'm sorry if I'm being nosey, Lenny, but I have to ask. What changed your mind about the treatment?"

"I had to be around to watch Lillian grow," he said, as if that was the obvious answer. "I wish you had brought her."

I wasn't sure what to think about Lenny's response, but I squeezed him even tighter.

"Me too. I'll make sure you meet her. Don't you worry. She's perfect. How did you and Sherri get here?"

"That charming fella right over there," he said, pointing to Athun, who was seated next to Sherri. I said hi to Sherri before I made my way over to Athun.

"I love you so much," I told him in his ear, as I hugged him.

"And I love you so much more," he whispered back.

Next, I hugged Maura, my parents and Weston's other siblings until I was back by Weston.

"Cora," I heard Lenny call.

"Yes?"

"This restaurant has fiddleheads. Did you know that?"

Oh, Lenny.

"I can't wait to try them."

Lenny's smile was so broad, I could see all his false teeth now. I leaned into Weston.

"You did all this for me?"

I didn't understand the correlation here. *Why would my parents or Lenny need to be here to hear Athun's news?*

"I'd do anything for you."

My heart, it's doing this flip flop thing again. It's this weird sensation I've grown to love so much. Is it Weston's words or the way he looks at me when he says them that has me believing everything he says?

We ordered our meals and conversed as we ate. I lost count of how many times I looked up at everyone seated at the table and felt whole. I finally felt whole again.

"Excuse me everyone," Weston said, standing up.

What is he doing?

"I haven't even made it through my meal yet, which is delicious by the way, but I'm sitting here nervous as hell. I feel like I should've written a speech or something because I don't really know how this goes," he said, looking down at me nervously and smiling. "But here we go...

Cora, as you've probably caught on by now, I've invited everyone closest to us out to dinner tonight so they could share this special moment with us. Yes, I'm about to propose to you, but as you know, my feelings don't flow from my heart to my mouth as freely as yours do. So know, when I'm saying these words to you, they are feelings I've burrowed deep down for some time."

My heart was already melting and he hadn't even begun to say what he wanted to. He took a deep breath to shake the nerves and began again.

"The day you knocked on my door was one of the weirdest days of my life. I was becoming an introvert, skipping out on our family's Easter dinner and being glad Olivia had lice so I could use that as an excuse to stay home and sulk in my own self-pity. I didn't like seeing my own family and not because I didn't love them dearly, because I do. I'd just get the same questions like "What's new?" and "How are you and Olivia?"

Before I met you, the answers to those questions weren't good. I was still waking up every morning without meaning. When you stepped into the house that day and you had a look around, I'll admit I watched your every move. It was clear to me that you were sad. I felt an overwhelming need to know your sadness, which is why I asked you questions that were too personal for answers. I can still remember at one point, your body started to tremble and you caught yourself because you didn't want me to see how broken you were. I realized right then you were just as lost as I was and I felt compelled to help you when I didn't even know how to help myself.

It didn't take long to realize I was falling for you and it was incredibly hard to sit back and watch you fall for someone else. Sometimes I found myself so drawn to you, I had to leave the room. My heart was conflicted. I tried to rush things that night I kissed you, but what a fool I was to think I could turn off emotions with the flick of a switch. The truth is, I thought that was it, I had lost my chance, but to my surprise, you held on. Thank you for never giving up on me. Thank you for being patient with my silence and knowing I needed to work out my own heartache.

My family is here tonight. I hope they ask me what's new after I shut up with this speech so I can tell them why I feel like the luckiest man in this room. I hope they ask me how Olivia and I are doing. Well, I obviously am doing great," he laughed, "but

Olivia is doing even better and I owe all that to you.

I've come to know your facial expressions quite well. I know what they mean and how you're feeling. The night you told me you were pregnant, well I must admit that was the ultimate shocker, but I'll never forget the look on your face and what that did to me. You didn't think I could take it. You thought that would push me away. You were used to being let down, given up on and made to feel forgettable. I scooped you up into my arms and held you because I wanted you to see I was never going to be the man that you could push away. I didn't want to let you down because you're not forgettable...you're unforgettable.

Cora, I can promise you with all my heart, your future with me will never equal your past. I love you and I don't deserve you," he said, shaking his head. "Will you marry me?"

Weston got down on one knee and opened another black box. This time, it had a different ring in it. A rose gold band with a solitaire diamond. He began laughing and now I was laughing too. Not only was that the most amount of emotions I've ever heard Weston speak at one time, but here he was again, telling me he'd like me to propose to him and then he steals my thunder.

"You couldn't wait?" I laughed.

"I couldn't wait, Cora. You were meant for me."

It was then that I heard everyone around the table clapping and cheering for us, but I didn't look away from Weston's gaze.

"Yes. My answer is yes."

THE END

EPILOGUE

Lenny just finished his treatment and the latest results show no sign of cancer. I don't visit him or Sherri as often as I'd like, but we talk on the phone and I stop by the nursing home with the girls when I can.

Athun and Maura talk on the phone every day, multiple times a day. I haven't seen Athun this happy in some time. I swear any day now he's going to tell me he is moving to California. The long distance seems to be agonizing. He tells me how special Maura is, but I already know. I couldn't think of a sweeter person for Athun to swoon over.

My mom and dad have morphed into grandparents quite nicely. They bought a swing set for Olivia and we walk to their house several nights a week for dinner. Nothing is better than having your parents for neighbors.

Olivia is starting Kindergarten next year, so I began teaching her her uppercase letters and how to write them. She's just about perfected how to write her name now. Weston keeps insisting I can put Olivia into pre-school where she'd learn all of this stuff, but I enjoy teaching her and the time we spend together. Besides, she loves being at home to dote on her little sister.

Lillian is the sweetest baby I could ever ask for. She smiles constantly and has just started to laugh. She's still sleeping in our bedroom, but not for long. She's almost sleeping through the night and then I'll move her into her own room. I'll miss her, but I'll also enjoy cuddling up to Weston again every night.

Weston is an amazing father. The other night he told me how he had always wanted another child, but never imagining that dream becoming a reality. He thanked me for giving him Lily. I enjoy watching him pour his love onto both the girls. We are all so lucky to have him and I count my blessings each and every day.

Weston is letting my mother-in-law, well, ex mother-in-law, stay at his other home until she figures out where she wants to live. I think she'll stay here, though. She enjoys us just as much as we enjoy having her.

Then there is me. Gosh, do I love me. Can one actually admit that they enjoy the person they've become? I love my family. I stop and admire them constantly. I still pinch myself sometimes. Is this real? Right now I'm planning a small intimate wedding to take place in our backyard this spring. How did I come so far in such little time? I'm so free. Free. A simple, four-letter word I never thought would apply to me. And yet, it does. I am beyond grateful.

ABOUT THE AUTHOR

Born on October 1, 1987, in Boston, Massachusetts, I grew up in Plymouth where I was encouraged to write in my very first diary given to me by my mother at age nine. It was then I found my love for writing. I still reside on the east coast with my husband, five children and several farm animals. When I'm not typing away on my keyboard, you can find me in the kitchen cooking up something delicious! I also love crafting, gardening, reading, spending time with my family, venturing outdoors and camping.

I love to hear from readers via comments or emails. I answer personally at this e-mail address:

indiegirld.duquette@gmail.com

You can also add me on Facebook, @AuthorD.Duquette

Made in the USA
Columbia, SC
05 August 2022

64667039R00139